CALLBACK

CALLBACK

BY
GINGER FRIEDMAN

LIMELIGHT EDITIONS
NEW YORK

First Limelight Edition/May 1996

Grateful acknowledgment is made for permission to reprint from *A Doll's House* by Christopher Hampton. Published by Samuel French as a Samuel French Ltd. Edition. All rights whatsoever in this play are strictly reserved and application for performance etc., should be made before rehearsal to Casarotto Ramsay Ltd., National House 60-66 Wardour Street, London, WIV 3HP. No performance may be given unless a license has been obtained.

Published by Proscenium Publishers Inc., New York

Manufactured in the United States of America

Library of Congress Catalog-in-Publication Data

Friedman, Ginger.
    Callback : how to prepare for the callback to succeed in getting the part / Ginger Howard Friedman — 1st Limelight ed.
       p.   cm.
    Originally published: New York : Bantam Books, c1993.
    ISBN 0-87910-077-X (pa)
     1. Acting—Auditions. I. Title.
PN2071.A92F75 1996
792'.028'023—dc20   96-14055
                                   CIP

In loving memory of Robert Carroll White
For Keith—lifelong friend and fellow passionate theater lover
For Michael—my mentor
For Carol, Helayne, Hope, Lillian, Raphaela, and Renee—such special
women
For Kevin who brings out the funny in me
For Kathy Berman—a true goddess who keeps me and my loved
ones nutritionally correct
and
For Joe—my hero

CONTENTS

CONTENTS

CONTENTS

PART 2: CREATIVE VISUALIZATION FOR THE CHARACTER

"You'll know they *have it* the minute they walk out onstage, or you'll think your watch has stopped!"

Ethel Barrymore
—as an auditor for an actor's scholarship audition

INTRODUCTION

In the life of an actor, getting a callback is crucial. You are one step closer to being hired. Without a callback you have no chance of being hired. A callback is your second audition for a production, which means that you gave a winning audition the first time and you are being "called back" to be seen again. You are being seriously considered for the part.

At the callback you must demonstrate to the auditors (playwright, director, casting director, producer) that you can sustain your performance and that your first one wasn't a fluke! In fact, too many actors fail at the callback because of poor preparation or in most cases no preparation at all. This book covers, in detail, how to succeed at the callback through intelligent preparation. As a professional casting director, I firmly believe that if you gave a good first audition, there is no reason in the world to fail when asked to repeat it.

You must also prove to the auditors that you fit well into the ensemble, as perhaps it was only the casting director who initially screened you at the first audition; the director, playwright, and producer will probably see you only at the callback. And when you get a callback, you are to be heartily congratulated because you obviously gave a winning audition. Now, after you've patted yourself on the back, keep this in mind: *It is not good enough to get a callback.*

When you get a callback, be assured that there are others being called back to read again for the same part. Let us assume there are ten actors, including yourself, who have been chosen to read a second time for the same character. You've got one chance in ten to get the part, which of course is the same chance the other actors have. Do you consider these to be good odds? As a professional casting director, I don't. All ten actors gave fine first readings and all were in the right ballpark, typewise. One of you will be offered the part. This book is about what you can do to make sure that it is *you* they are referring to when they proclaim, "There's no contest; this is *the one!*" At the very least, you should be invited to the second callback, if there is one after a process of elimination at the first callback.

By the conclusion of the first round of auditions, often at least one actor's reading was so dynamic and extraordinary that the director will declare that actor to be "the one." Therefore, his picture and resumé will be ceremoniously placed on top of those of the nine actors who gave those fine readings and will also get callbacks.

"The one" might not even be the type originally wanted, but his acting at the audition was unrivaled. The astute director understands that talent becomes type during the rehearsal process, or the type originally sought after will be changed to accommodate "the one."

If "the one" sustains his brilliance at the callback, the part will be his. In a way, he has already gotten the part! The actor has no knowledge of the commotion brought on by his reading and that there is no contest—unless his second reading falls short of the first one. He has to be extraordinary just one more time.

Ah, but there's the rub. Most actors fail at callbacks! Even "the ones" who give those powerful, intelligent, and appealing first readings often fail. This book will show you

how creative visualization will *prevent* you from failing at
your auditions and your callbacks.

Several years ago, I introduced the students in my New
York "How to Audition" workshops to the art and act of
projecting and visualizing the future of the characters'
lives and the future of the actors' professional lives.

First, we work on creating the history and background
of the character, concentrating on important events leading up to the confrontation in the dialogue on the audition
sides (*sides* are a section of a scene from the script given
to the actor at the audition). Then we work on the "here
and now," meaning what is being said by the characters,
the actions taking place, and also what is *not* being said.
Finally, we work on the future, which must exist in and
emanate from the mind of the actor. If the actor, through
creative visualization and projection, is making choices—
what I think of as all-important, "life-or-death" choices—
for the character's future based on the actor's very
personal fantasies, visions, imagery, and dreams during
the preparation, the performance becomes more powerful, alive, and formidable. And the actor, because of the
higher stakes and added stimulation, communicates more
and therefore is more appealing and exciting to watch and
listen to. The actor must have a commitment to and an
investment in the future welfare of the character he or she
is auditioning for. (In the visualization examples in Chapter 4, I'll refer to this commitment and investment as what
the actor is "fighting" for.) This is the stuff that callbacks
are made of.

There is a preponderance of dull and lifeless work
done at the cold-reading auditions (also referred to as prepared readings) that simply should not occur; you have
time to go over the sides and make all sorts of powerful,
incisive, and profound choices, the best of which derives
from using creative visualization. The application of this
tool adds vivacity and life to the readings. In creative
visualization, there are no obstacles, losses, or defeats. It's
fantasy time all the way. You project your future exactly as

you want it to be with no detours, boundaries, or constraints. This applies not only to your choices for the characters but to choices regarding your personal goals as an actor.

We will work on two kinds of creative visualization in this book. Part I introduces creative visualization *for you to apply as actor* as you plan your personal goals for success, starting before the initial audition and continuing throughout the audition process. Part II introduces creative visualization *for your characters* as you prepare to perform at the audition. Covered fully are intelligent planning and strategies for getting the callback; focusing on the interview; auditioning for the director; preparing for success; auditioning in an office for the agent and casting director; being brilliant despite an inferior reader; auditioning for a familiar script, for comedy, commercials, soaps and sitcoms, film, and theater; the ice-cold reading; looking out for your interests; and finally, the power of the actor.

I have seen the magic taking place with my students when they apply creative visualization to their audition preparation. I have rejoiced when former students let me know how creative visualization played a major part in their being hired. I am overjoyed to learn from an actor that until he or she used creative visualization, there were no callbacks—and suddenly there were! Enough time has elapsed since I began my instructions in creative visualization to conclude that the results are nothing short of spectacular.

In recent years the principles of creative visualization have been accepted by people of science. Mainstream physicians practicing at esteemed universities and institutions have incorporated this powerful modality into their practices and teachings. Athletes have depended on help from this technique to enhance their skills. "Inner tennis" has been around for more than a couple of decades. Seminars on creative visualization are presented in the boardrooms of Fortune 500 companies. It is time for the actor to reap the benefits and rewards.

In creative visualization, we intentionally cause to

come into being that which evolves from our thoughts, imagination, wishes, and fantasies.

It is not enough to use your imagination to visualize and project your future as you wish it to be unless you actively pursue it also. I have seen people make a stab at it and think only good and pure thoughts concerning their future, but then sit and wait for it to happen. This is not the proper application of the principles of creative visualization. To achieve a successful outcome, one must not deny the negative aspects of one's situation, because only by acknowledging the harsh realities can we change negatives to positives. Thinking good, pure, and happy thoughts makes little sense if we don't apply and take action and perform deeds to create a happy ending.

The true practitioner and devotee of creative visualization understands that positive thinking equals positive action. And that means getting off your butt and going out there and making your dreams come true. Reality is built from dreams. As an example, I will share an experience from my own life.

My survival job when I was making audition rounds was modeling. One day, as I was checking the directory in the lobby of a building whose occupants were dress designers with showrooms, a very chic woman approached me and asked if I was looking for work. I replied that I was. She instructed me to follow her, and a voice in me said to do so. She took me upstairs and into the dressing room of a large and attractive showroom, flung a dress at me, and said, "Put this on, come out and model it. If you can make this dress look good, you got a job." She left me there holding a black taffeta, belted, short-sleeved horror of a dress. I held it up for further inspection and decided that this was the ugliest dress I had ever seen in my entire life. How was I going to make this monstrosity look good? I put it on and although it was a perfect fit, it did nothing for me and I did even less for it. But I wanted and needed that job so badly I could taste it.

I knew it would take monumental effort to prance around that showroom with grace and pride, and I worried that my acting skills would not suffice. Somehow, I had to look great and feel great in that black aberration, so I made the decision to imagine that I was wearing the most beautiful dress ever created. I stepped away from the mirror and closed my eyes. I created my dress. It was a powder-blue chiffon strapless cocktail dress studded with tiny seed pearls and diamonds cascading from the bodice down one side of the billowing skirt—a Ginger Rogers dancing dress, very glamorous, very expensive. With this image, I left the dressing room and proceeded to the showroom and to the mystery woman. I walked about and turned and modeled my heart out in my glorious dress.

Suddenly the woman yelled out, "My God! You've done it. You actually made that dress look good. You're hired!"

This was my first creative visualization experience. And this is how I became a model for this wonderful and talented woman, Anne Klein.

In the average scene study class, actors are taught "naturalistic" acting. It squelches the possibility of pre-Stanislavski, soap opera, or early Hollywood acting. "Feeling" is stressed in classroom instruction, but too often strong communication between the characters and the actor's commitment to the relationship between the characters is sadly downplayed. A lot of self-indulgence and emotional masturbation mars the performances of actors who've taken such classes. I'm not saying that good teaching and good work isn't being done in these classes. I am saying that the teaching and the work is not taken far enough. And, unfortunately, unfinished work still in the practice stage is what the auditor often sees at the audition. The performances are not stageworthy because the actor is playing off a half-truth; the actor is not encouraged to make strong enough personal choices for the character and fails to make a powerful enough commitment to the relationship between the two characters. Therefore, communication on the stage is poor, which is dull to watch. This kind of work might look good in class but most definitely dissipates onstage. It doesn't survive the trip; it dies. Please remember that what looks good in many acting classes frequently perishes on an audition stage. This book will offer solutions to this problem, including the use of creative visualization.

As part of their training, acting students should be performing full-length plays, not just scenes. They should be directed by professional directors and also taught how to survive with an inept director during the rehearsal process. When I offer scene study classes, I always include professional guest directors to direct my students in all the scenes they do for their classroom work. Rehearsal technique is an integral part of scene study. Actors should be playing before live audiences, even if they're just friends and relatives. We always wind up the scene study semester by presenting the best of the work to an invited audience made up of those friends, relatives, agents, and casting directors.

Some teachers do not take into account that the actor will perform one day to a house full of strangers where people in the last row of the balcony must be reached to be a part of the event. The audience member is not a spectator but a participant! No one goes to the theater to see you. People go to see themselves—through you! This means that you must be emotionally accessible to them.

Most acting teachers certainly do not respect the audition; indeed Mr. Stanislavski himself would be turning over in his grave if he knew what actors must go through and what is expected of them at this thing called the audition!

You know your audition was successful when you are told you are getting a callback. Often, however, you will be satisfied with your performance at the audition but will not get a callback. In many instances, this self-evaluation is totally justified. Occasionally, an actor whose audition performance outrivals and surpasses everyone else's still won't get hired for the part because of an inbalance in the casting regarding age or height, or because the actor's personality and stage presence are too strong in comparison to the star or other actors in the ensemble. Wonderful actors have had musical numbers cut at the request and often demand of the star of the production during rehearsal because they were showing signs of perhaps having the show-stopping number. I have even seen actors fired from a production because they were threatening to the star! This should not be a dilemma for the actor at the audition. Give all your strengths and take the risk.

You should not have to depend on the auditor's response to determine your level of competence and artistry, although dedicated and serious actors never think of themselves as being great at their craft. The audience and critics acclaim and celebrate the magnificence of the actor's performance. The actor, while emerging triumphantly, will simply proclaim that "it felt good." However, in an audition you should have the capacity and expertise to analyze and critique yourself with fierce and brutal honesty so you suffer no delusions and fallacies about your work. If you truly "failed" at your audition, you should be aware of what you might have done wrong. Many actors are not proficient in self-evaluation, and without such skills they cannot effectively prepare for auditions and callbacks. The actor often hangs on every look, word, phrase, and gesture the auditor delivers.

This book will teach you the technique of evaluating your performance at the audition.

An actress recently lamented to me after her callback that the casting director responded to her performance by telling her how nice it was to see her again, addressing her by her name. I told her that I thought his response was friendly and positive, but she insisted that his words were the kiss of death, even though she admitted that she thought she did very well. She complained that he didn't compliment her performance, but instead just said how nice it was to see her again. She was flabbergasted the next day when she was called and told she had gotten the part!

If it's compliments you want, stay home and allow your family and loved ones to shower you with words of acclamation and praise. The only compliment you should want to hear from the auditor is, "You got the part!"

The most beautiful words in the language to an actor are: "You got the audition," "You got a callback," and "You got the part."

You can't get the part unless you succeed at the callback. You won't get a callback unless you know *how* and *when* to prepare for it, and you won't get the audition unless you are prepared, knowledgeable, and aggressive. Creative visualization will help you to succeed.

The time to prepare for your callback is at your *first* audition, after you have created a history and background of yourself as character, and after you have created the important events dealing with the here and now. Then you will be ready for creative visualization of your character's future.

I will lay the groundwork for you so that you can get the audition, get the callback, and get the part.

The time to prepare for success in your career and life is *now*.

PART 1

Creative Visualization for the Actor: Stage Smarts and Screen Smarts

THE COLD READING

Creative Visualization Exercise:
BEFORE THE FIRST (INITIAL) AUDITION

On the day of your initial audition, just before you leave home, sit in a comfortable chair with your legs stretched out in a relaxed position. Make sure your shoes are comfortable or remove them. Allow your arms to rest at your sides or on the arms of the chair. Make sure the room is quiet and devoid of activity and people. Close your eyes. Breathe slowly and deeply five times and then see yourself at the audition (this preparation and relaxation is how you will begin *all* the creative visualization exercises in this book). It doesn't matter if you are not yet privy to the dialogue, the relationship between the characters, or the physical layout of the audition space. Just project a vision of taking charge of the stage with your emotional power and strong communication skills. Focus on what you do know about the character. See yourself reading effectively and finishing the reading triumphantly. See the auditors' faces beaming and thanking you gratefully, not courteously. Visualize getting a message saying you got a callback! Project into the future and see how getting this part will enhance your life and your career. Personalize everything and be liberal with your visualization. Visualize your glow as you leave the audition knowing that you gave a powerful, honest, and appealing performance. Visualize yourself onstage or screen performing this part, with great success.

Now, let's take action and make it happen. Go to your audition.

AMOUNT OF TIME FOR PREPARATION

When you arrive for your audition appointment, check in with the monitor and pick up your audition sides. Arrive about thirty-five minutes before your scheduled appointment.

You should not begin your preparation for the cold-reading audition until twenty minutes to a half hour before your appointment. Your first instincts and choices made for your character will be your strongest ones, and you should stay with them. If you give yourself hours—or even a single hour—to prepare for three or four pages of dialogue, at some point during all that time you will probably discard at least one of your choices, erroneously believing you can come up with a better one. You will be abandoning the instincts on which your strongest choices are based, and you will be defeating yourself. The choices must be powerful and very personal and should be put to use as soon as possible after you've come up with them. It is best to work against a deadline, which will force you to employ your original choices. Also, if you give yourself an hour or longer, you will probably complete your preparation within a half hour anyway, and then you will be sitting around waiting to be called and one by one your choices will dissipate. You don't "own" the material yet. Several minutes after your audition, it will leave you. You won't "own" it until you have been hired, completed the rehearsal process, and are performing it eight times a week or are in the final "take" or a shoot.

The ideal situation for you is to prepare, get right out there, and do it immediately. Ask the monitor if the audition will take place on time and gauge from his reply when you should begin your preparation. If you pick up your audition sides a day in advance, I advise you to do no more than read them once and put them out of sight until a half hour before your appointment. You can think about the character, but don't start making those life-and-death choices so far in advance. Once you create your reality as character, you want to get right out there while your inner life choices (the personal choices you make for your character that are not given by the playwright) are fresh, honest, and alive.

Prepare by using the character's vocabulary, not the actor's. By this I mean get right into first-person character, and as you make your choices, don't make them as an actor making them for your character, make them as you, the character. As an example, do not say, "What is my character fighting for from the other character?" Say, "What do I desperately need from [the other character]?"

You must get into character from the very beginning to avoid holding your character at arm's length. Work from the inside, making choices from your head, your world, and your perceptions to avoid the possibility of intellectualizing and making outside judgments about the character. It is the thoughts within you as character that should be leading you to your feelings as character. If you talk about your character, you are not aware of his or her feelings.

You can't depend on the playwright or screenwriter because all he gives you are words. You don't know what is in his head, world, or perception, and second-guessing will only interfere with your preparation. He writes half a play. The playwright's play. You, the actor, must write your half, the more important half where the honesty and vulnerability is. The inner life and interpretation is up to you.

What is not on the page is the most important part of

the character and script. You know how we sometimes do not divulge our real feelings and thoughts because we are protecting ourselves and simply cannot expose our vulnerability? Well, the characters in plays and screenplays do the same thing when it comes to the words. Sometimes the writer has the character lie, just as we do in life at times without the help of a writer. You must service the playwright's and screenwriter's play and create a play within the play.

Your character must come alive through *you*, through *your* emotions and sensibilities, your frame of reference, your attitudes, your mannerisms, your idiosyncrasies, your character. First of all, that person on the page is only a printed word! There is no such person! You are going to bring that printed image to life! (I tell my male students that this is the closest they will ever come to giving birth!)

Don't put a lid on your emotions. Do not ever make the choice that you don't want the other character to know how you really feel. If you make such a choice, there will be no emotional reach-out or action and emotional power. What you hide from the other character you hide from the auditors. You will be cheating your character and therefore yourself. Turn yourself inside out and work off your inner life and vulnerabilities while you are speaking the writer's words. You don't want to alienate the auditors. The other character will respond to your dialogue. Allow us, the audience, to respond to your emotions. Allow us to come close to you as you expose your true feelings of love, need, and vulnerability through honest and open communication about what's going on inside you.

I recommend that you have three items with you at all cold-reading auditions. The first is a medium-size notebook; the second, pencils and erasers; and the third, a small dictionary.

After you have checked in with the monitor and get your sides, proceed to the wall of your choice. Start preparing a half hour in advance. Unencumber yourself of overcoats and bags by placing them in front of you on the floor. Take a minute or two for breathing and relaxation exercises, and then begin.

Lean your sides on your opened notebook and have a pencil in hand. You already know the name of the character you are auditioning for, and it is now time for you to learn the name of the other character in the scene, which should immediately reveal the gender. Have the character breakdown with you during your preparation to refer to if you forget who the other characters are.

Before you begin to read the sides, say to yourself as character, "Today is the most important day in my life. [The other character] is the most important person in my life." Ask yourself (as character) why today is the most important day in your life. The answer, which is the same for any scene you will ever be auditioning for, is, "Today is the most important day in my life because today is the day that I've got to change my life and [the other character] has got to help me." I urge you to use the words, "has got" instead of "is going" because there is more of a sense of desperation and action. Remember, the word is desperation, not desolation. You will be starting with a strong sense of immediacy, importance, relationship, and positivism—all of which are vital if you are going to communicate a strong stage presence to the auditor from the very first word of your dialogue.

Start to read your audition sides (including the stage directions) slowly and with your strongest concentration. As you read, jot down on the pad what you consider to be salient bits of your character's dialogue spoken and even some responses from the other character, if you wish. You will be writing the highlights, the dialogue that shoots up at you from the pages. You may paraphrase. There is no need to write a complete line of dialogue as written by the writer. Write only what seems to be important to you and in your own words (you'll see some examples of this beginning on page 15). By the time you reach the final page, you should have about six, twelve, or fifteen lines written.

You may also jot down reminders to yourself on the audition sides such as, "Yell at him here" or "Reach out and touch him gently" or "Recoil from his slap" and so on. (Of course, a real slap, kick, punch, or other violent action should never be executed during an audition. A mishap could occur. If a stage direction tells you to physically assault the other character, you should slap the air in front of the reader's face. Before you begin your reading, tell the person of your plan to do this. If you are the one to be assaulted, ask the reader before you begin kindly not to slap you.)

Put the audition sides down and work off the lines on your pad. You've read the sides once and once is enough —if you concentrated fully on what you were reading. Reading them more than once wastes precious time and is not necessary. You see, you don't have to burden yourself with making choices for every word. You will be thoroughly servicing the writer's script because your choices will emerge from the highlights of your dialogue. You've written the most important lines and the most powerful things your character says—according to your judgment —and you are the most important person at the audition.

Now, create a history and background for yourself as character starting from the day the character was born. Make as many choices as you can from your own background as long as they don't conflict with the character on the page. For example, if you are auditioning for the part of Billie Dawn from *Born Yesterday* and you, the actress, were born into a well-to-do family and you are college-educated, you must discard your background and create another one more fitting for yourself as Billie, a culturally and educationally deprived person.

There is no need or time to write your choices down. They will stay with you as you continue your preparation, and they will still be with you during your performance at the reading.

Use whatever you choose to use given by the writer and add from your life, creating past events that are based on real-life experiences. If need be, add to your character's background anything that does not come from personal experience but that seems to make sense to you. After all, these are events that *could* have been part of your character's background. Find the character in you; he or she is there!

If I were to ask you where you were born, what your cultural, economic, ethnic, and spiritual background is, and what your relationship was like with your folks, your siblings, your peers, teachers, lovers, and so on, you could answer all those questions. So you must for every character you will audition for. Create your reality from the day you, the character, were born, including all the highlights of your character's life up to this day and all the important events leading up to today's confrontation. Always think of the material on the audition sides as a *confrontation* between the characters, not conversation. You've got to make what I call life-and-death choices for your character and create conflict where there is none on the page; therefore, confrontation is much stronger than conversation.

Don't dwell on your past. Create one event and go right on to the next. Do this until you get to where you decide where you met the other character, then start to make more detailed choices. The scene is always about you and the person to whom you are talking.

If there is a word on the page you don't understand, look it up in your dictionary. If it's not in your small edition (you certainly don't want to carry a heavy and thick volume around with you) perhaps the monitor can help you out with the meaning or pronunciation. If you can't get help, give the word any meaning you want and pronounce it your way.

HOW TO PREPARE FOR THE COLD READING

EXAMPLE: A *Doll's House*
by Henrik Ibsen,
a new version by Christopher Hampton

We will begin to prepare for the callback—which starts with the preparation for the cold reading and leads us right into creative visualization to use as character.

In this example, the audition sides are presented first as written by the playwright, followed by the actor's choice of highlights in the dialogue. You will see how the highlights are extracted from the original two-character scene. This is a scene between Nora and Torvald Helmer. They are married and she has decided to leave him.

Nora: Sit down. This is going to take some time. I have a lot of things to say to you.

Helmer: (Sits opposite her, on the other side of the table.) You worry me, Nora. I don't understand you.

Nora: No, that's just it. You don't understand me. And I never understood you . . . until this evening. No, you're not to interrupt me. Just listen to what I have to say. . . . This is a reckoning, Torvald.

Helmer: What do you mean?

Nora: (After a short silence.) Does anything strike you about the way we're sitting here now?

Helmer: No, what?

Nora: We've been married now for eight years. Don't you think it's significant that this is the first time you and I as husband and wife have sat down to have a serious talk?

Helmer: What do you mean, serious?

Nora: For eight whole years . . . no, longer than that, from the time we first knew each other, we've never exchanged once serious word on a serious subject.

Helmer: Do you think I should have continually bothered you with all sorts of problems you couldn't possibly have helped me to cope with?

Nora: I'm not talking about your problems. What I'm saying is that we've never sat down and talked and tried to get to the bottom of anything together.

Helmer: But, Nora dear, what good would it do you if we did?

Nora: That's exactly what I mean. You've never understood me. I've been treated very unjustly, Torvald. First by Daddy, and then by you.

Helmer: What do you mean? The two of us have loved you more than anyone else in the world.

Nora: (Shaking her head.) You've never loved me. You just enjoyed being in love with me.

Helmer: Nora, what is all this?

Nora: It's true, Torvald. When I lived at home with Daddy, he fed me all his opinions, until they became my opinions. Or if they didn't, I kept quiet about it, because I knew he wouldn't have liked it. He used to call me his doll-child, and he played with me the way I used to play with my dolls. And when I moved into your house . . .

Helmer: That's no way to describe our marriage.

Nora: (Unperturbed.) All right, when Daddy handed me over to you. You arranged everything according to your taste, and I adapted my taste to yours. Or perhaps I just pretended to, I don't know. Probably a mixture of both, sometimes one, sometimes the other. Now, looking back, I feel as if I've lived a beggar's life—from hand to mouth. I've made my living doing tricks for you, Torvald. And that's what you wanted. You and Daddy have done me great harm. It's your fault I've never come to anything.

Helmer: Nora, how can you be so unreasonable and ungrateful? You've been happy here, haven't you?

Nora: No, never. I thought I was. But I never have been.

Helmer: Not . . . happy!

Nora: No. Cheerful, that's all. You've always been
           very kind to me. But our house has never been any-
           thing but a playroom. I've been your doll-wife, just
           as I was Daddy's doll-child when I was at home. My
           children as well, they've been my dolls. I used to
           enjoy it when you played games with me, just as
           they enjoyed it when I played games with them.
           That's all our marriage has been, Torvald.

Helmer: There's some truth in what you say, however
           exaggerated and hysterical it may be. But from now
           on all that's going to change. Playtime is over; now
           it's time you were educated.

Nora: Who? Me or the children?

Helmer: You AND the children, Nora, my love.

Nora: Oh, Torvald, you're not the man to teach me
           how to be the right wife for you.

Helmer: How can you say that?

Nora: And as for me . . . what makes me qualified
           to bring up children?

Helmer: Nora!

Nora: After all, you said it yourself just now—you
           said you couldn't take the risk.

Helmer: That was in the heat of the moment! You
           mustn't take any notice of that.

Nora: No, what you said was quite right. I'm not
           qualified. There's something I have to achieve first.
           I have to educate myself. And you're not the man to
           help me with that. I have to do it by myself. That's
           why I'm leaving you.

Helmer: (Jumping to his feet.) What did you say?

Nora: I must stand on my own two feet if I'm to un-
           derstand myself and the things that are going on
           around me. That's why I can't stay in your house
           any longer.

Helmer: Nora, Nora!

Nora: I'm leaving right away. Kristine will put me up
           for the night. . . .

Helmer: Are you mad? You'll do no such thing! I for-
           bid you to!

Nora: It's no use you forbidding me to do anything now. I'll take what belongs to me. I don't want anything from you, now or ever.

Helmer: But this is madness!

Nora: I'm going home tomorrow . . . I mean, back to my old home. It'll be easier for me to find something to do there.

Helmer: It's only lack of experience that makes you so blind. . . .

Nora: Experience is something I have to find, Torvald.

Helmer: You can't abandon your home, your husband, and your children! What do you think people will say?

Nora: I can't go worrying about that. All I know is that it's something I have to do.

Helmer: But this is outrageous. It's going back on your most sacred duties.

Nora: And what in your opinion are my most sacred duties?

Helmer: Surely you don't have to ask me that. I mean your duties to your husband and your children.

Nora: I have other duties which are just as sacred.

Helmer: No, you haven't. What, for example?

Nora: My duties to myself.

Helmer: Before anything else, you're a wife and a mother.

Nora: I don't believe that anymore. I believe that before anything else, I'm a human being, just as much of one as you are . . . or at least I'm going to try to turn myself into one. I know most people would say you were right, Torvald, and I know you'd be backed up by all sorts of books. But what most people say and what you find in books just doesn't satisfy me anymore. I want to think everything out for myself and make my own decisions.

Helmer: You don't seem to understand your position in your own home. There's an infallible guide in this sort of situation, you know. There's your religion, what about that?

Nora: Oh, Torvald, I really don't know what religion is.

Helmer: What are you trying to say?

Nora: All I know is what Pastor Hansen told me, when I was confirmed. He told me religion was this, religion was that. When I've got out of all this and I'm on my own, I'll be able to think the whole thing over. I want to see whether the things Pastor Hansen told me are true, or at any rate whether they're true for me.

Helmer: But that kind of thing is unheard of for a young woman! Well, if you refuse to be guided by your religion, at least let me appeal to your conscience. I suppose you do have some sort of moral code? Or perhaps you don't? Mm?

Nora: Well, Torvald, it's not a very easy question to answer. I really don't know. I find it all quite bewildering. The only thing I do know is that my opinions about these things are quite different from yours. I've also found out that the law is different from what I thought. What I can't accept is that the law is right. That a woman shouldn't be allowed to avoid hurting her old, dying father or save her husband's life. I won't accept that.

Helmer: Don't be so childish. You don't understand the first thing about the society you're living in.

Nora: No, I don't. That's why I want to make myself part of it. Then I'll be able to make up my mind which of us is right—society or me.

Helmer: I think you must be ill, Nora. Feverish. You seem to have lost your senses.

Nora: I've never felt as convinced and as lucid as I am tonight.

Helmer: You're convinced and lucid and you're abandoning your husband and children. . . .

Nora: Yes. That's right.

Helmer: Then there's only one possible explanation.

Nora: What's that?

Helmer: You don't love me anymore.

Nora: That's exactly it.

Helmer: Nora! How can you say that?

Nora: It hurts me very much to say it, Torvald, you've always been so kind to me. But there's nothing I can do about it. I don't love you anymore.

THE HIGHLIGHTS OF THE DIALOGUE FOR NORA

Below, I have extracted what I perceive to be the highlights of the dialogue for Nora. You might want to check over the scene once more after reading these notes (I've done the same highlighting for Helmer, following the analysis of Nora's character) to see if you would choose differently. What *you* consider to be the highlights *are* the highlights—for you! (Note: When you are making choices for your character, do not attempt to get into the thought process of the other character[s] in the scene. Leave that to the actor[s] who are reading for those parts. Focus on *your character in relation to the other character*, since the day they first met each other.)

I have a lot of things to say to you.

We've never understood each other. This is a reckoning.

In eight years of marriage we have never sat down and exchanged one serious word on a serious subject.

I've been treated unjustly. You've never loved me—just enjoyed being in love with me.

Daddy treated me as a doll-child and when he handed me over to you, you arranged everything according to your taste. I feel as if I've lived a beggar's life—from hand to mouth and doing tricks for you. It's your fault I've never come to anything.

Our marriage has been a game.

You can't teach me how to be the right wife for you.

I have to educate myself. That's why I'm leaving you.

I don't want anything from you, now or ever.

Before anything else, I'm a human being. I want to
  make my own decisions.
I cannot accept that a woman has no legal rights—as I
  have been denied.
It hurts to say it but I don't love you anymore.

Let's summarize what the playwright has given us.
Nora, you are telling your husband of eight years, Helmer, that you are going to leave him. You explain that you
have never once in your marriage sat and discussed anything important together and you feel that you've been
treated very unjustly by your father and then by your
husband, both of whom treated you like a doll-child. Helmer is shocked to hear your words. You explain how you
never came to anything because of them. Helmer can't
believe that you have not been happy with him. He admits that there might be some truth in what you say and
declares that things are going to change. He says that you
and the children will be educated. You tell him that he is
not the man to teach you how to be the right wife for him.
And you admit that you are not qualified to bring up their
children. He had even mentioned that earlier, but now he
pleads that it was said in the heat of the moment. We must
assume that he had been berating you for something. You
say that you must educate yourself and that is why you are
leaving him. He is devastated and forbids you to go, but
you tell him that you will leave the following morning. He
begs you not to leave, but you say that your duties to
yourself are most sacred, not toward your husband, God,
or your children. You bring up the question of the law,
which prohibits a woman's rights. You finally admit that
you do not love him anymore.

This summary is for the purpose of explaining what you
can gather from just one reading of the sides and writing
down the highlights. You do not necessarily have to sum
up for yourself what you've gotten from the sides when
you are at the audition and preparing. I am doing it here
for you for practice purposes.

So far, in our preparation, we have dealt with only the words on the pages. We've got the bones. Now we have to add the flesh and blood. After you have written the highlights and quickly summarized what you've been given to work with, you should begin to create your character's history and background. For our purposes, there is a beginning, middle, and end on those sides; and as far as we are concerned, we have the entire play. Forget about what is on the pages *not* given to you. Concentrate only on these pages. We will "write" our play within the play. Do not actually take the time to write—create in your head, and when you have completed making your choices for your character, it is time to get into that audition room and perform at once. Selecting the highlights and summarizing are the first part of our preparation for Nora.

The following is an example of what your choices and preparation could be for Nora:

I was born in _____. (Unless you are familiar with a Scandinavian town, choose the town you were born in for the audition. When you get the part, you will then do research on Nora's proper birthplace.) My father was a doctor and my mother, a housewife. (Remember, we are going to make choices based on just the pages given to us; therefore, we do not know what her father's occupation was so we will create what we *feel* could be appropriate.) My mother was a gentle and passive woman. My father showered me with affection and toys and made me feel like a princess. I was privately tutored at home in reading, some arithmetic, history, art, and music. I had very few friends and no relationships with men until I was introduced to Torvald nine years ago by an associate of my father. Torvald courted me and asked me to marry him. I loved him dearly and he was so good to me, just as my father had been, and so we were married. Life with him was wonderful. He looked out for my every need and made all decisions so I wouldn't be burdened. We had two children, and I felt as if I was actually one of his children instead of his wife. But I had no complaints. Life was fun and filled with games, toys, and laughter. However, about a year or so ago, I began to feel frustrated about who I was and how I had been treated by my husband. I felt as if I had not reached adulthood even though I had a husband and children and ran a home. I was made to feel as if I were still a child, and I suddenly wanted to know what it felt like to be a desired and respected woman. Then my father took ill and there were some papers I wanted to sign as his legal caretaker that would have benefitted us all, but I was told that I was not allowed to sign them because I was a woman! Torvald was in total agreement, and that immediately caused a distance between us. For the first time in my life I began to ponder my existence fully, and when I realized how shallow my life was, I made up my mind that a drastic change must take place. I decided to leave Torvald and go out on my own, and now I must tell him why I am leaving. I simply cannot just walk out on him. After all, he has been my husband for eight years and is the father of my children, and I feel he did the best he could and thought he was acting in my interest all along. But he is a bully and thinks of me as a stupid child. I must convey to him why it is that I must leave, and when I tell him that I don't love him anymore, it really hurts me to say it—because in reality, I do love him and only wish that he could change and grow with me. I will say anything I can to shock him into understanding and learning what it is I must have from him in order to stay. I'm fighting for him to love me enough to do anything to keep me with him. I'm fighting for the rest of my life, and I am fighting for him.

These are your inner life choices—the play within the play. These choices do not come from the playwright. You have now created a full character from the playwright's words on the pages and from your personal choices for the character. This is the second phase of our preparation for Nora. We are not yet finished, but let's go on to Helmer, and afterwards we will pull it all together.

THE HIGHLIGHTS OF THE DIALOGUE FOR HELMER

I'm worried. Nora is acting strangely.

She's complaining that we've never exchanged a serious word, but I never wanted to bother her with problems that she wouldn't be able to solve anyway.

I'm sure we have loved each other dearly no matter what she is saying.

She is describing our marriage in a most horrible way.

She is now being unreasonable and ungrateful, and I thought she was always happy.

I am willing to make changes to accommodate her wishes.

I will educate her and the children.

She is rejecting me and wants to leave, but I forbid her to.

She must be mad or blind. She can't abandon me and her children. What will people say?

She has sacred duties to us. Before anything else, she is a wife and a mother.

She is rejecting her religion. I must appeal to her moral code.

She must be ill and feverish.

I fear she does not love me anymore.

The following is an example of what your choices and preparation could be for Helmer:

I was born in [same instruction as with Nora]. My father was an attorney and quite strict with me. He

ruled the household and provided for our every
need. My mother did all the womanly things around
the house and was kind and loving to me, especially
when my father wasn't around. He admonished her
for being too soft with me and turning me into a
sissy. I always tried to please him with my endeav-
ors, but he always demanded more of me no matter
how well I did. I am an attorney as my father was. I
met Nora at a Christmas gathering of family and
friends. I took to her immediately and called on her.
It didn't take long for me to ask her father for her
hand in marriage, and he consented. We've had a
perfect marriage for eight years with two wonderful
children. I've loved her dearly and provided everything for her and the children. I made sure that she
never had to be involved with anything taxing. To be
sure, she would not have been able to make any
decisions on anything of consequence. She had always been shielded from the harsh world outside of
her home. So naturally, I carried the burden regarding important decisions, which any good husband
should do for his wife. But lately I noticed some
discontent in Nora and it bothered me. We even had
some words where I was forced to tell her to continue to just be who she was and not to ask questions or worry her pretty little head about things she
could do nothing about. She is so childlike. In a way
she is more like my child than my wife. But she has
always been such fun to have near me. Now she is
telling me that we have never sat down to have a
serious talk, which, of course, I know, but now it
appears she is complaining about it. I explained to
her that it would do no good because she could not
have helped me to cope with problems anyway. She
accuses me and her father of treating her unjustly,
but we have loved her more than anyone else in the
world. She is being unreasonable and ungrateful.
She's blaming me that she's never come to anything.
She says she has never been happy with me. So I
admit maybe there is some truth to what she is say-

ing and I promise that I will change all that and will educate her and the children to the ways of the world. But she tells me that I am not the man to teach her how to be the right wife. She admits that she is not qualified to raise her own children, which I had told her in the heat of the moment when we had our words earlier, and then she says she is leaving me! I forbid her to, but she says it's no use, she is leaving and wants nothing from me. I tell her it is her lack of experience that makes her so blind, and she says that it is experience that she must find. I tell her that she can't abandon me, her home, and her children without caring what people will say. She says she can't worry about that. I plead with her about her most sacred duties. She says her duties to herself are just as sacred. I mention her religion and her sense of conscience. She says her opinions about these things are quite different from mine. I fear that she might be ill and feverish, but she says she's never felt as lucid as she now does. I accuse her of not loving me anymore, and she admits that that is true. She tells me that she does not love me anymore. I am in a panic. I cannot lose my love. I feel that I am dying from her words. What will I do without her? What will people say? I am willing to do anything to keep her. I am fighting for her to love me and stay with me. I am fighting for my very life!

I did not depend on the playwright to establish the inner lives of Nora and Helmer. The playwright has given you all he's got to give: the words—the least important part—and for a cold-reading audition, you do not change one of them! You have "written" (in your head) your half of the play. The more important half! The half with the vulnerability, humanity, and honesty.

CREATIVE VISUALIZATION
A DOLL'S HOUSE (CONTINUED)

THE LAST PART OF YOUR PREPARATION IMMEDIATELY BEFORE YOUR INITIAL COLD-READING AUDITION

You are now going to take the next step to assure yourself of not only getting a callback but being "the one." We will start with Nora.

Nora, you have spoken your last words to Helmer during this confrontation. You know what you desperately want from him: his true love, so that he will want to change and grow with you. Then you will be able to have a life filled with love, respect, companionship, and passion with your husband.

If you could have anything you want, Nora, what would you want to happen right now between the two of you immediately following the conversation you and he just had?

Do you want him to say, "Nora, I never realized

that you felt this way. I only wanted to care for you and protect you from the harsh world. Please forgive me. Stay with me and I promise to change."

Yes, this is what you would love to hear. You are so much in love with him. You told him that you don't love him anymore, but actually you still do and it hurts you deeply that you would have to leave him. You told him this untruth to shock him into the reality of what you are about to do. And now he responds to you, and his words are exactly what you had hoped they would be. You stay and the two of you continue to talk throughout the night about your feelings, frustrations, and needs. He listens and understands and appreciates all that you tell him. The two of you talk of the future and how things will change in the marriage. You want a certain amount of independence. You want to study and learn. He swears his support and encouragement. Finally, you both go to your bedroom, and for the very first time in your marriage, lovemaking for you is filled with passion and gratification. As a matter of fact, it is the first time that he displays such passion and expertise as a lover.

So far I can think of nothing that you, the actress, could not find acceptable. Let's continue. I am asking you, the actress, if you had a choice to take a holiday anywhere in the world, where would you love to go? Nora, that is where you go with your husband. Visualize yourself there in that wonderful place with your man. As actress, personalize and substitute your Helmer. Use your own husband or boyfriend or someone you wish was your husband or boyfriend. Have him in your mind's eye all the while during your preparation and as much as possible during the reading. (Your reader might be very unattractive to you.)

Nora, you finally have an equal partnership in your relationship with your husband, your sex life is fulfilling, you are learning the ways of the world, your opinions are asked for and respected, you travel to beautiful places, and your life is secure, happy, and filled with love. Can you, the actress, relate to this? I would think so. However, perhaps you do not have children and as a matter of fact, you have no desire to be married. In this case, substitute your own private choices. In other words, lose Nora's children and the marriage and instead make other choices. I want you to make choices not only that you are comfortable with but that are meaningful to you. When you get cast as Nora, during the rehearsals you will have to find a way to *justify* being a wife and mother. But for now, *this* is what you are fighting for this night as you are telling Helmer that you are leaving him!

    Helmer, if you could have anything you wanted immediately after this confrontation with your wife, what would it be? I think you certainly would want her to come to her senses and realize that she loves you, needs you, and will never leave you. This seems the perfectly obvious choice. Now, what are you willing to bring to the table? I would like you to be open enough to consider the possibility that perhaps you might need to alter some of your ways to accommodate Nora. What would they be? Perhaps you might want to discuss certain things with her and ask her opinions. Wouldn't it be nice if you discovered that she is a quick learner and that she actually has an intelligence far exceeding anything you imagined? It might be a little off-putting to you; after all, you are not accustomed to sharing insights with your wife, and maybe you just liked feeling that you were more intelligent and therefore superior. Well, make a discovery that when she displays a bright and original mind, a very interesting phenomenon occurs. You actually become sexually aroused by her. That night, when you both retire to your bedroom, you make love to her, and for the first time, you feel you are making love with a mature and sensuous woman, and this is the most excitement you have ever felt. Unlike before, she is actively participating as a love partner in bed.

She becomes a true companion to you in every way. I assume that you, as actor, can relate to this. She contributes feedback regarding your business and things even improve there. If you, the actor, cannot relate to being an attorney, please choose a profession that you would be more comfortable in. As an actor in a production, you must do research about your characters, including the type of work they do, but for the audition and especially for the callback and creative visualization process, you should personalize and substitute. There is no time to do all that background work, and it belongs in the rehearsal.

So now, Helmer, you have a truly wonderful marriage filled with excitement and love, and your work is more rewarding than ever before.

This is what you are fighting for as Nora is telling you that she is leaving you.

The amount of time spent on creative visualization for the character at the audition should probably take about two or three minutes. If you are not called in to read within moments after you have completed your preparation, continue to centralize yourself within the character and focus on a moment or two of the character's history and background. Then return to the here and now as character, concentrating for a few moments on the highlights of the confrontation between the two characters, and then going on to the future as you wish it to be. Keep going through this cycle until they call you in, making sure that as you proceed into the audition room, you are heavily involved with the creative visualization.

Do not make the mistake that some actors do by dismissing all their thoughts about the character and events when they have a lengthy wait after their preparation. Their rationalization is that their choices will stay put without forcing them to do so and when called upon some time later, they will spring forth! The opposite is true! You will lose them. Remember, you don't own the character, choices, and events on the pages until you have thoroughly rehearsed the part. They dissipate after a few minutes.

CHAPTER THREE

IMMEDIATELY AFTER THE FIRST AUDITION

Preparing to Succeed at the Callback

Most actors don't remember anything about the scene or character they audition for after a day goes by. You can be told you are getting a callback one day later or thirty days later. Your first reaction upon being given the news is exaltation. And why not? You have every right to be overjoyed. What is your second reaction? Fear? Panic? Yes indeed! The stakes have just become higher, which causes terror, anxiety, and horror to set in. Let's keep the first reaction and throw away the second.

The main reason why actors experience fear and panic is that they fail to remember the important things about the first audition. This inability to remember is one of two major reasons why actors fail at the callback.

The second reason is that when actors are given a callback, they erroneously believe they must improve and deliver a better audition at the callback. This belief will most certainly sabotage the second reading. How can you make a circle any rounder when in fact it is already a circle? How can you make a straight line any straighter? If you try, you will only muck it up. Leave it alone! I'm from the "If it's not broken, don't fix it" school. Repeat your winning performance! Don't try to improve it!

When your initial reading is over and you hand back the sides, the first thing you should do to prepare for a successful callback is to sit down somewhere—right there, in the outer office, outer lobby, backstage hallway, or wherever—and take out your notebook and pencil and begin to write, staying in character and *writing in first-person character*, what just transpired in this confrontation between you, as character, and the other character. Write in your character's words, not the playwright's. Don't confine yourself to your character's actual dialogue. Paraphrase and substitute the words for your character. Write about your (character's) feelings about the relationship and the events and what you were fighting for from the other person. Write whatever comes to your mind. Free associate. Just let your mind go and allow the words to flow. Keep writing until there is nothing left to write. The amount of time expended on the writing should be five to ten minutes.

Now, as *actor*, evaluate your reading. Write down your feelings about the scene, relationship, and events and what might have been a difficulty for you. If you were dissatisfied with something you did in the reading or if you could or should have done something different, write it down.

Maybe you felt you didn't fight hard enough for what you needed from the other character, leaving the performance weak. This could indicate that your choices might not have been strong enough to begin with. You realize that next time you must apply yourself more diligently in this area. Or perhaps you weren't really able to justify why you said something to the other person. It didn't ring true to you; therefore, you feel it was totally false in your performance. If you get the callback, you know you must and will do that part better.

You are analyzing your performance so that you can be aware of your weaknesses. By being aware of your acting problems at the audition, you are able to eliminate your weaknesses and present strong, honest, and dynamic readings.

I just exhorted you to repeat your performance, not improve it. In other words, do not prepare for the callback by wanting to do the entire scene better or differently. You must realize that whatever you did, they liked it! However, if to your way of thinking you didn't justify an event or a line or two well, you certainly may correct it in your callback reading. I just don't want you to go in with your mind set to give a different reading. You will be defeating yourself.

After you complete your notes, write what you wore, including your jewelry, accessories, undergarments, perfume, or cologne. Wear the same outfit, from head to toe, to the callback for two reasons. The first one is for yourself. You want to get back in character as you were the first time, and the same outfit will help you significantly. The second reason is for the director, who only remembers you from what you wore and cannot be convinced that you are the same actor if you have another outfit on.

The time you invest writing your notes after your audition is time well spent. That night before going to sleep, make sure that the last thing you do is to read the pages you wrote and then place them in your night table drawer. Happy dreams.

YOU GOT A CALLBACK

When your phone rings a few days later and you are told that you got a callback, indulge in your exaltation. Later, when you begin to feel the pangs of panic, stop and think that in your night table drawer lie the passwords to guide you through your callback. Get them out and read them, and you will once more be immersed in the scene. The panic will subside—the joy will prevail.

You will be told if the entire script is being made available to you and where to pick it up. Obviously, you will be curious to read the script to see how many lines you have and to learn more about your character.

Do not allow your knowledge of the entire script to sabotage your second reading. You will now be aware of all the events from page one to the end. You should consider the few pages presented to you at the callback to be the entire play. Remember, there is a beginning, a middle, and an end on those few sides. Don't dissipate the action on those pages by incorporating and playing off events in other parts of the script. You didn't read the entire script the first time and you got a callback! You don't have to read it now either. If your curiosity wins, remember my advice. The character doesn't know what happens after this scene, so you don't have to know either. And the choices you made during your preparation the first time with no knowledge of what took place before or after the scene were fine. Do it again.

Creative Visualization Exercise: THE DAY OF THE CALLBACK

The best time to do your creative visualization is before you leave for your audition. It makes no difference what time of day it is. Try to make it the last activity before the audition.

Read your notes once more. Prepare yourself for creative visualization (as you did in the first exercise on page 3) by sitting in a comfortable chair, relaxing, and breathing deeply and slowly five times. Close your eyes. See yourself at the audition. You are very well informed about the character, the dialogue, and the relationship between the characters. Be that character. Perform the scene and see yourself up there mesmerizing a row of auditors with your presence, appeal, intelligence, and emotional power. Visualize being told that you got the part.

Now go to the callback audition with confidence.

At the audition give yourself the same amount of time to prepare as you did the first time. If you are given the same scene to do, refer to the highlights that you wrote down on your pad.

If you are given another scene, write a new set of highlights from the pages and make your choices from them. After you have completed your preparation, begin to visualize your future as character, repeating from the first time or altering it to fit the new scene.

You might be asked to read more than one scene with no preparation. Don't worry. You no longer need time to work on the character and relationship. If the scene is from another part of the script and with another character, just ask the auditor to tell you one thing about the other character. You are involved in character enough to handle the situation.

You may be asked to stay around for a while so that you can read with several actors. Therefore, never make another appointment on the day of your callback until at least three hours after your appointment. If they ask you to stay, this is a very good sign. They like you and want to see other actors play off you. This is how they pair actors and hire them. You might get shuffled around and asked to stand in a line, then to change places several times. They are looking again in this way for compatibility. Sometimes they don't make decisions after the callback, so a second one is arranged. The strongest candidates return to read once more and to be viewed and shuffled. This can be frustrating to the actor, especially if it is a third or fourth callback! Please be positive and know that you are one of the best actors around. Even if you don't get the part after several callbacks for one production, I can assure you that if you've come this far, your day will come.

YOU GOT THE PART

Congratulations!

Usually the news arrives via telephone from your agent or manager. If you have no representation, the call will come from the producer or casting director. Choices have been made, and you are one of the winners. It is certainly a time for celebration. You earned it. You will now embark on one of life's glorious adventures. See you opening night.

INTELLIGENT PLANNING AND STRATEGIES FOR GETTING THE CALLBACK

Creative Visualization Exercise: "CLEANING HOUSE"

What would you like to change about your life? Your relationships, your survival job, your personal habits (eating, sleeping, smoking, etc.), your living conditions, your acting classes (or lack of), and the general manner in which you conduct your day-to-day life?

Prepare yourself for creative visualization. Visualize ridding yourself of all things (one at a time) that contribute negatively to your life. Be brutally honest. See what's left. You are "cleaning house." Visualize cutting out people who do nothing to enhance your life. Let go of arrangements and relationships that inhibit you. Change your personal habits. You know how many hours of sleep you should get, you know what good nutrition is, and you certainly know that smoking can damage your health and your energy level. You are fighting for your future. Visualize yourself rearranging things in your life that will make a positive impact on your future. Erase all things from your life that could sabotage your future and delay it. See yourself not being afraid to allow someone to help you in your endeavor. Get to the point where you start to feel better about yourself and your life. If you can get to that point, then you have every right to feel wonderful about yourself.

Now, how about putting some of these fantasies to work for you and actually doing what you must do to enhance your life? When if not now?

THE INTERVIEW

You are your own audition at the interview!

You don't have sides to read. You aren't playing a character from a play or a film. You are showcasing yourself using your words. You're playing yourself. The auditors are interested in observing your every move, facial expression, and general demeanor. You are, in fact, auditioning.

Interviews are frequently held by many theater and film directors, agents, managers, and occasionally by top casting directors. For them the purpose of the interview is to learn who you are by talking with you, listening to you, and observing your mannerisms and attitudes. The goal of the interview for the auditor is to discover a person interesting and appealing enough to warrant an audition. The goal of the actor during the interview is to be such a person.

Don't be surprised if the following occurs at your interview: The interviewer sits across a desk from you and looks at your picture and resumé. Then he puts it down, looks at you, and says, "So, tell me what experience you've had in acting."

You and he both know that he just read the answer to his question on your resumé, but what you should also understand is he simply does not know how to conduct a proper interview; therefore, you must learn how to call the shots during this important procedure so that you do not allow his ineptness to sabotage your interview!

Because you are your own audition, there must be a script. To prepare for your future interviews, create your script. Sit down and write the highlights of your life since you were a child. Include your personal convictions, attitudes, and things you are passionate about. Keep your dissertation as positive as possible with few or no complaints. Do not feel obliged to restrict your writing to the subject of acting. You are a whole person; your resumé speaks for your training and experience. Venture beyond the world of acting with observations pertaining to life around you. Memorize your script, and during an interview, draw on your writings as you wish. Obviously, you are not going to perform a recitation. It is there only if you need it and if you are able to naturally incorporate a section or two into the conversation. Be prepared to deviate from it.

Do your research before the interview takes place so you will know what you are being interviewed for. Far too many actors show up for their interview and the first question they ask the interviewer is, "What am I being interviewed for? Is it a play or a film?"

I don't consider this to be professional behavior on the part of the actor. Your agent or manager can supply you with some background details. A phone call to the producer's or casting director's office can get you some answers. The character breakdown in the actor's trade paper gives you information. Find out something about the character you are being interviewed for. Ask what his or her economic, cultural, and ethnic background is and where the locale is. Ask if it is a period or contemporary piece. Ask if it is a comedy or drama. Dress accordingly but not in a costume. Choose from your closet what most gives you the feeling of what the character might wear. If it is impossible to gather any information or if it is an informational or general interview being offered to expand the actors' files in the casting department of the producers' office, an agency or a theater company, wear your most flattering daytime outfit.

Bring the right personality. When the actor doesn't do some background work, the entire interview can go down the toilet. I was casting a melodrama-mystery film, and the director requested interviews to be set up. We were looking for an actor to play a troubled male character whose dark side was very prevalent. One actor being interviewed for this part had just done a Comet cleanser commercial a day or so before, and what he brought to us was his Comet personality. He never deviated from his upbeat, smiling, happy self, which was not what we were looking for. Do not spend the entire time with us skulking and being sullen, but do show us that you have those qualities.

If you know that the character is an Italian from Brooklyn, give us half a minute of Brooklyn Italian. If the character is a Wasp from Connecticut, give us half a minute of Connecticut lockjaw!

Please do not try to be funny at the interview if you know that nobody falls down the steps laughing over your humor. Don't play it for laughs. If you are positive that you are a genuinely funny person, please bring your humor to the interview. It is a strength of yours, so by all means, use it. One thing is for sure—the auditor can always use a good laugh! And generally, we like people who make us laugh.

Creative Visualization Exercise: THE INTERVIEW

Before you leave for your interview, take ten minutes. (Please arrange your life so that you are never rushing about to make your appointments.) Prepare yourself for creative visualization. Visualize yourself at the interview, even if you are not familiar with the surroundings you will be in during your interview. Place yourself in an office across the desk from the interviewer, using a substitute person if you don't know who your interviewer will be. You are talking freely and openly. The interviewer is engrossed in your every word. You are telling him amusing anecdotes about yourself and others—extracts from your dissertation and perhaps something that recently occurred that is very well worth telling. You are asking questions about the production. You are discussing a movie you just saw that greatly impressed you. You ask him to tell you about a place he's been to that you are interested in, or you are asking him where he bought his sweater (only if you truly love the sweater). You are conducting yourself beautifully, you feel great, and at the conclusion, an audition appointment is scheduled.

Go to your interview. Be on time. Relax and enjoy the experience.

THE AUDITOR

The auditor is your first audience and a most formidable one. He wants to like you no matter how much you may insist (and you do constantly) that he is your enemy. Of course, he is not your friend either. He was hired to do a job and one hopes that he does it with perception, wisdom, and affability. When you are auditioning not for a production but for an agent, you will probably be expected to perform a monologue. The agent needs to see your work before he can submit you to the casting director. Once you get submitted and then accepted by the casting director to audition for the production, you will probably read from the script (although many auditors request monologues); at the callback, you will also read from the script.

Please be aware that agents cannot get you an audition! They can only submit you to the casting director, the one who gives you an audition. If the casting director is not interested in seeing the agent's submission, no appointment will be scheduled.

Recently, a Tony Award winner was interviewed on television and was asked if her agent got her the part. The actress replied yes, but in truth, this is not so. The actress got the part. The agent submitted her, the casting director granted her the audition, the director chose her, and the producer hired her. She got the part because her reading was extraordinary. Her agent had nothing to do with that except to acknowledge that he had a very special actress for a client.

Directors call the shots at the audition. I don't want you to think of them as an enigmatic force. I want you to see them as normal human beings with flaws. Directors have a tremendous burden not only directing actors but auditioning them, choosing them, and assembling their technical staffs. Directors run the show. And they receive the credit for a hit and the blame for a failure.

More often than not there will be no introductions, so don't expect them. Time is money and introductions are time-consuming. Do not take it upon yourself to reach out to shake hands. You have probably been announced by the monitor (the person you check in with and get your sides from) and your name is next on the audition schedule for the day.

Beware of the friendly auditor who says more than, "Hello, whenever you are ready." You don't want an overly social auditor who finds it necessary to hold a chummy conversation with you immediately before your audition. You have just put in your time preparing, and you are trying to stay in character. What do you suppose will happen to all those choices you made for your character if there is a two- or three-minute tête-à-tête? Everything you planned is going to go right down the drain. You must not allow this to happen. If you fail at an audition, it is never anybody's fault but your own!

If the auditor is beginning to get involved with you in a conversation, simply ask (do not tell) if you could possibly do your audition first and then talk because you fear you will lose what you've prepared. Of course, you convey this request in your most humble and amiable manner.

The auditor should be aware of his transgression, but

don't count on it. He might be somewhat abashed by your request, so make sure that your reading is so powerful that it cancels out his dander. Better to throw him off center a little than to throw away your entire preparation and fail at the reading. During your encounter with auditors before and during an audition, your tension is heightened and you require more time to recapture the feelings of yourself as character. Protect yourself; no one else will!

You may encounter the director who feels obliged to offer you every detail of the plot. You've done your preparation on your own, and you are not asking him to share this information with you. You wish he would just shut up, sit down, and allow you to do your stuff! All that information is just going to confuse you, and none of it is reflected on the sides. So all you can do is listen while you hold tightly to your own choices!

Some directors will approach you as you begin your reading and tell you what they are looking for. Once again, listen, holding on to your choices and adding something of theirs to your reading. Do not rid yourself of what you did in your preparation. But allow them to see that you can take direction by incorporating some of their input into the reading.

There is a very famous Hollywood actor who has directed plays in New York. In one such play I was involved with, I watched in horror as he approached each actor as they were ushered one at a time into the studio and he stood nose to nose (literally) while telling what he expected in the reading. He slowed down the entire procedure, frightening many of the actors so that most of the readings were way off kilter.

Directors too often don't know how to conduct themselves professionally during auditions. They may send out messages to the actor that are contrary to their actual feelings about the reading. A director and I were auditioning actors for an off-Broadway play. An actress was about one-third into her reading when the director abruptly stopped her, coldly thanked her, and asked for the next actress to be sent in. I was extremely impressed with what I considered to be an intelligent, exciting, and highly appealing reading, so I was surprised that the director didn't like her. But as soon as she was out of the room, he turned to me and exclaimed with great glee, "Wasn't she just marvelous? I think she's the one!" I certainly agreed and asked him why he ended her reading so abruptly. His reply was that he could see that she was perfect for the part, so why waste his time? Throwing professionalism to the wind, I jumped out of my seat, ran after her, stopping her just as she was about to step into the elevator, and told her what the director had just said. I didn't want her to leave feeling she had failed. I also told her that she would be getting a callback—something an auditor should not normally tell the actor right after the reading. The reason for this is that even though it might be said in sincerity at the moment, by the time the auditors have seen all the actors, they probably will have given other callbacks. If the auditors consider enough of the later performers to be better, they will eliminate some originally considered. It's all right to tell the actor if callbacks are being scheduled for the next day or two and it is agreed that all actors giving a great audition will automatically be asked to come back. Most of the time, however, auditors need three or four weeks to see all the actors for a Broadway or off-Broadway play or a film; callbacks are saved until everyone has been seen, and then the director is very selective.

I have been at the side of directors at many auditions in my career as casting director (and once as playwright), and I have been confused by the mixed messages they send out to the actor at the conclusion of his reading. Some exclaim how wonderful the reading was and even ask the actor if he would be available for a callback the following week. Naturally, actors float on air after hearing these words and would gladly cancel a European trip to be available for the callback. But as the actor leaves, the director puts his picture and resumé on the "no" pile! I have learned not to automatically put the actor's name on the callback list without first confirming with the director that his response in front of the actor was genuine.

When I have asked these directors why they compliment actors after bad performances, they have given such answers as, "I never know what to say to them" or "I like to make them feel good when they leave the theater." And indeed you do feel good, but after several weeks go by and you haven't heard from us about that callback that you "knew" you were going to get, you become confused and despondent.

The appropriate and professional conduct on the part of the director should consist of a simple "thank you" to you after your reading; then the director should confer privately with his colleagues after you leave. It would be lovely if directors who truly love your reading would communicate it to you; some will, but don't count on it. And besides, what good would it do you if you don't know whether they are even being sincere? So be prepared to be stopped in the middle of your reading. Most directors will certainly stop you when they don't like what you are doing, and they are within their right to do so.

When an auditor loves your reading, the usual comment when you have left is something like, "I don't know how he got it or where he got it but I love it!" I've heard countless variations of this reaction. Some (not many) pinpoint specifically, in a most eloquent fashion, why a reading was good or not good. Many auditors, even upon threat of torture, could not articulate an intelligent evaluation and a constructive critique of your performance.

I would like to share with you the exchange that took place between a director and his two A.D.'s (assistant directors) during auditions for an off-Broadway play I was casting. Several actors had auditioned for us and we were going over their head shots.

Director:	I sort of like this one. What do you think?
A.D. #1:	I don't know. Well, sort of.
A.D. #2:	I think I loved him, kinda.
Director:	I liked this one, or did I?
A.D. #1:	I didn't. I like this other one. He's cuter.
A.D. #2:	You think he's cute? Gee, I don't.
Director:	What about this one? I loved him.
A.D. #1:	I didn't love him at all.

A.D. #2:   How can you say that? I thought he was
            great, sort of.
Director: Do you like this one better than that one?
A.D. #1:   Gee, I don't know. I kinda liked them both.
A.D. #2:   How about this other one. I loved him. I
            would like to get to know him.
Director: I wouldn't. He's not my type. I seem to
            recall there was another one I liked best but I can't
            remember which one it was. Do any of you know
            who it was?

If this kind of behavior hasn't driven me from theater,
nothing will.

I am grateful for the wise, perceptive, and organized
directors I've had the pleasure to work with.

Another form of blatant dishonesty often takes place,
but it is the actor who is guilty. When I set up appointments with actors to audition for a production, I usually
do so through their agents. I also make callback appointments through their agents. It is an uncomfortable chore
listening to an agent insist that an actor whom we did *not*
choose reported that we loved his reading and told the
agent he would be getting a callback, when in fact this is
not the truth.

As casting director on the project, I know exactly what
takes place at every audition. A casting director is paid by
the producer but works for the director. I sit at the director's side along with the A.D. and the playwright, or I sit
directly behind the director. (This is true when casting for
theater and film. In a television audition the director is
seldom present).

The casting director knows what is going on during the
auditions, so please do not hear compliments when they
are not given. You are doing yourself a vast disservice.
And you can only fool your agent for a short period of
time.

When I am teaching, I work on preparation for the
cold reading and rehearsals for the monologue audition. I
teach my acting students how to make the strongest and
most interesting choices they can for their characters and

how to develop emotional commitment to the character and to the relationship between the two characters in the scene. We work on strong communication, emotional "reach-out," emotional action on the stage, and the inner life of the character, as well as on the dialogue that is *not* on the pages. This work gives the actor a strong stage presence, making us, the auditors, believe everything the actor is saying and making us want more of him. These classes are referred to as process-oriented classes.

When I am casting a production, I look for a strong stage presence without concerning myself with how the actor arrived at it. The audition is a result-oriented situation. I cannot and will not share my critique with the actor after he has auditioned because I am representing the production, not the actor, and there is no time to provide feedback when hundreds of actors are to be seen. To tell you the truth, under these conditions, my colleagues and I have no further interest in an actor who has presented inferior work.

All auditors are result-oriented, and most don't know why the reading was good or bad or why they loved you or not. They do not get involved with concerns about your preparation for the audition. It is essential that *you* understand that the choices you made for your character and your preparation will determine the outcome of your performance.

One more word about directors. Many will conduct the audition with intelligence, civility, and dignity. Just remember, the auditor is *always* rooting for you. Even the "mixed message" ones. They *want* you to be wonderful, but some are too enthusiastic with their praises.

Creative Visualization Exercise: AUDITIONING FOR THE DIRECTOR

Who is your favorite director? Film or theater, it doesn't matter. I want you to audition for that director right now.

Set yourself up properly for creative visualization and

then "see" your director. If you are not familiar with his face, then see the productions that you so admire because of this director. See the scenes and the actors performing. See yourself as one of them. Visualize yourself playing the part of your choice. Immerse yourself in it.

Now you are going to audition for that part before the person who directed those actors. He is out there watching you, but you can't see the face in the darkness before you in the theater or studio where the audition is taking place. But he is there watching you, that great director whom you so admire and long to be directed by. You *are* acting for him now. He is auditioning *you*! Perform that part as you remember it. Improvise. Create your dialogue and use whatever dialogue you remember. Create the scene and the relationship between the characters. Your favorite director is watching. When you finish, I want you to hear a voice in the dark before you, saying your name and telling you that your reading was extraordinary. He is usually economical with his praise, but when he speaks, it is the truth!

Doesn't it feel wonderful? This is the way it feels when you *do* audition for someone you admire. Do this exercise often using different films and plays. Audition for your heros. First in creative visualization. Next—in reality!

SELLING YOURSELF— THE BASICS

Art has to be sold. It's as simple as that. If you are a professional actor or acting student, you are in business, and it is yourself you are marketing. You are the artist and the art. You have created a salable commodity—yourself —with a little guidance, nurturing, direction, and inspiration along the way from your teachers and heroes.

No one, not an agent or manager, can market you as well as *you* can, and I must inform you that early in your career, no one wants to sell or buy you! Be aware of the harsh reality but do not allow yourself to be discouraged. Every star and working actor was once where you are. Someone's getting the work out there—it might as well be you. Make it be you! Fight like hell to get the work!

I take issue with anyone proclaiming that an actor got an audition, a part, or "made it" because he was at the right place at the right time. That actor was probably always at the right place. If you think good luck is out there waiting for you, wake up. Good luck is what you create for yourself. You've got to go out and make it happen. You've got to be your own good luck.

Perhaps you know of actors who "had connections" and that's how they got cast. With connections, it is obviously easier to get an audition, but there is no way that an actor is going to get beyond the audition if he or she does inferior work there.

Often during an interview, a star will state that he has been very lucky. This is modesty and humility talking. He is not about to publicly say that he fought like a tiger and came through with excellent work, but he knows what he went through and he is perfectly aware that luck didn't play the significant role in his climb to stardom. He worked his butt off and paid his dues to make it.

You have to pay your dues—literally and figuratively—before you can support yourself as an actor. This means that until you are accepted as a card-carrying, paying member of the professional actors' unions—SAG (Screen Actor's Guild), AEA (Actor's Equity Association) for theater, and AFTRA (American Federation of Television and Radio Artists)—you've got to prepare yourself properly to become a professional actor.

Are you receiving or have you had proper training? Auditors and agents want to know that you have studied with good teachers, and they look for this on your resumé.

If you are one of those people who believes you have "raw talent" requiring no training, you are in for a rude awakening. These people are crap-shoot actors who approach auditions haphazardly. This how-the-wind-blows technique betrays a lack of discipline. With no grounding or center, and with improper use of body and voice, they show their lack of professionalism. Because they are self-taught, which means they were trained by an amateur, they seem to have a block against learning from another person who, in their heads, is a threatening authority figure. I find these individuals unwilling to accept criticism and structure. They have no respect for process, which is what any good acting class works on.

Over the years, many have wanted to take my class as their first or only instruction. I do not accept such people into my audition workshops. I have in the past, but I have come to the conclusion that life is too short! These people are very seldom granted important auditions.

I do not accept actors who want to start their training with me, because that is doing it completely backwards. Mine should be the last class an actor takes. You've got to work on beginning technique and scene study before you are ready to think about working on acting for the audition. By the way, many fine actors, well trained and making a living through their acting, still continue classes throughout the years. Perhaps not every week—their schedules don't permit it—but in between plays or films, they "clean their base" by keeping in touch with a good acting teacher.

What are your personal goals? Are you more interested in film and television than theater? That's fine if you are, but where do you think all your favorite Hollywood stars, some of America's finest actors, started out? They didn't get famous until they studied with fine teachers, auditioned, got callbacks, were hired, and then appeared on stages, getting rave reviews that led them to Hollywood.

Remember the basics as you go about planning your professional life; you can achieve success if you make intelligent choices and prepare yourself properly.

Creative Visualization Exercise:
PREPARATION FOR SUCCESS

After setting yourself up for the exercise, focus on yourself as you are being told that you have gotten the part. Picture the scene as you wish to create it. You are signing the contract for Broadway, for a film or a miniseries, for the lead in a sitcom, or a major musical. Picture the events dealing with rehearsals, the shoot, or opening night. It's your cue. You're on! Be there. Indulge. The curtain has come down. Hear the thunderous applause. For you! Take your curtain calls. Or the film has opened and the preview audience is wild over your performance and you. Read the words of high praise from critics. Continue to project whatever fulfills your personal fantasies. This is your visualization and your life. Indulge yourself and enjoy this experience to the fullest. By the time you have completed your projection of your future, you should be experiencing an effervescent glow.

Do this exercise for the next couple of days to determine for yourself if you are on the right track in your organization and preparation for this career of yours. You will be stimulated because you are putting yourself in touch with your future as you wish it to be. Your motivation will be enhanced; therefore, your need to take action will be accelerated. Positive action on your part will bring you closer to your goals. Don't be concerned if your visualization varies or changes. This is how life works. It is important for you to understand and believe that you have the power to create your future with intelligently made choices to prepare yourself for success.

THE CASTING SYSTEM

Casting directors are no longer on the theater producer's payroll as they were years ago. They are hired on a freelance basis, production by production. Casting directors are on the payroll at major film studios, in network television, and at advertising agencies dealing with commercials.

As a freelance casting director, I am contacted by a producer interested in my services. Then I am given the script to read, details about preproduction and production dates, and other salient facts. If I don't have positive feelings about the material, I can't do my optimum work. Assuming I do like the play, a contract is drawn up between me and the producer. My services are required for several weeks, or perhaps years if I cast replacements and touring companies. The first few weeks are for preaudition work, which means rereading the script several times so that I am very familiar with each character and all the events. For each character I make a list of actors who I believe are in the right ballpark according to their type and acting abilities. I present this list to the playwright and director, requesting that each scratch any names not to their liking. Naturally, I will not call any of the scratched-off actors to audition for the play. However, after seeing every candidate, a part has not been cast, we sometimes have to reevaluate prejudices and bring in the actors we initially eliminated as a last resort. Ironically, these actors often get the part!

I always ask the playwright and director, "If you could have anyone in the world, dead or alive, to play each part, who would your first and second choices be?" I do not have the power to bring back dead actors. But their answers to this question reveal how each sees the character, and this is a great help to me. After all, I want to try to give them who they "think" they want, but I will also throw a few spitballs; I will deliberately have actors audition who might not be the type but whose work I am familiar with and whose talents I greatly admire.

Producers are notorious for seeking bankable actors. Directors and playwrights want the best actors, regardless of bankability. Producers want stars, and sometimes the star is lined up immediately, but sometimes I am responsible for tracking them down. When I am in charge of finding them, I usually do not bother going through their agents because by and large, agents do not want their star clients to work on Broadway. Stars make less money on Broadway than they do in film, and, of course, less for the client means less for the agent.

Many stars would relish the experience of returning to the stage once in a while. Some of them (not enough) periodically do return, accepting an enormous cut in fee, but they have the satisfaction of playing "live" where they feel they are "home."

The story is told about a script for a new play optioned for Broadway. It was sent at the request of the playwright to the agent of Henry Fonda, who indeed loved to return to the stage. The agent returned the script to the playwright with a note saying that Mr. Fonda was not interested in doing the part. When the play opened to wonderful reviews, Mr. Fonda went to see it. Afterwards he approached the playwright and asked why the part had not been offered to him. The playwright reminded him that he had sent it to him through his agent and he had turned it down. Mr. Fonda replied that his agent never gave him the script to read and didn't even mention it to him. The following day he fired his agent.

Some producers use a very cunning tactic when they are trying to create a star package for a play they want to produce. They will call a very bankable director and tell him that a superstar is definitely ready to sign. Then the producer will call the superstar and tell him that he has this top director signed. Names are mentioned to both parties. Each is impressed and highly interested. Despite proof to the contrary, producers think that stars can carry a play even if it gets bad notices.

I practice what I preach. When I say you have to be very aggressive, so must I when I am in pursuit. I rarely leave my apartment or office without at least one copy of the script I am currently casting because you never know who you will run into. Not that I would indiscriminately just hand it over to anyone, but certainly I want to be prepared if the right person comes along.

There I was, having lunch with a colleague at The Russian Tea Room, the famous New York restaurant frequented by celebrities, and before me at another table was the star I was instructed to find for the project I was working on. What to do! I had met her briefly at a party, but I knew she would not remember me. I wasn't in the mood to pretend we were old friends. I had pulled that one once and it worked. The star was too embarrassed to admit that he didn't know who the hell I was. But I was making such a fuss about (imaginary) past encounters with him that when I slipped him a script, he felt obliged to take it. On this day at The Russian Tea Room, I didn't want to be crass and interrupt the star's lunch, so I decided that after she finished eating and drinking, the logical next place she would visit would be the ladies' room. I sat in wait, silently chanting, "Drink-drink-drink more liquids." Finally, the moment arrived! She took her purse, excused herself from her lunch companion, and headed toward the back where the ladies' room was. I was up and out of my seat with script in hand right on her tail. She entered and I followed. I busied myself at the basin as she tended to her needs. When she emerged from a stall and came to a basin to rinse her hands, I turned to her and, feigning discovery that it was "she," introduced myself, proceeded to fill her in on the details of the production, and handed over the script as I officially offered her the part. She was so flustered that I was able to extract from her her California address and private phone number. To this day she does not know that this encounter in the ladies' room was not serendipity but planned.

One of the duties of the casting director is to prepare a character breakdown, that is, a description of each character. Copies are sent to all Actor's Equity Association franchised agents or to all Screen Actor's Guild franchised agents for film, along with rehearsal and production dates, the names of the principal people involved in the production, and, of course, whether cold readings or monologues are requested. Within a few days, agents submit their clients to the casting director with a covering letter suggesting which parts each client is being submitted for. Pictures and resumés are enclosed, which is helpful to the casting director. Of course, if the actor is well known, a

picture and resumé are not necessary. The casting director then chooses from these submissions the actors he or
she wants to see and calls the agents to set up the appointments. Agents try to sell all the actors they submitted, even if the casting director is not interested in some
of them. I am very pleased for the actors whom the agent
does this for because they are serving all their clients well
and are clearly supporting their talents. However, while it
isn't easy to resist, we must stay firm in our decisions. The
casting director always has sound reasons for rejecting
certain submissions. We know the actor's work and he is
short on humor; he is just plain too short or too tall; he
can't handle the heavy drama; he is on the director's "do
not want to see" list. Perhaps later these actors might have
to be seen when every possibility has been exhausted and
still the right actor has not been found.

The agent does not represent the production; therefore, he or she rarely sees more than the character breakdown. The agent is not privy to any insights into the
workings of the production except for what is made available to all actors on the breakdown, so when a casting
director rejects an agent's submissions, it is for a good
reason.

Audition appointments are made about five days in advance, but I've encountered many agents who do not contact their clients regarding the appointments until the
morning of the audition! When I have questioned agents
about this practice, I have gotten more or less the same
answer: "If I tell them a few days in advance, they'll only
forget." Would you forget? A professional actor is entitled
to know of an upcoming appointment. The agent main-
tains a certain amount of control over the actor this way.
And this reveals what some agents think of actors!

I also make appointments with actors from my files. I
rarely see an actor for a Broadway production whose picture and resumé arrive on my desk unsolicited (not submitted by an agent). If the picture and resumé catch my
eye and pique my interest, I have the actor audition with
a monologue in my casting office, but certainly not for the
production. I have to screen him first. My reputation is on

the line, and if I indiscriminately have untested actors brought before the director, playwright, and producer and they fail, I look as bad as the actors.

The first day of auditions arrives, and for the next few weeks we will be seeing perhaps a few hundred actors, depending on the project. Stars will be flown in from Los Angeles, Canada, England, and other places. Usually the producer flies them to New York first-class and sends them back on coach if they fail!

Each day of auditions, my office gives the auditors the audition schedule. The schedule is prepared in duplicate so that at the end of each day, a copy from each auditor is returned to me. The sheet includes the name of each actor, the time of the appointment, the actor's source (where he or she came from, plus the agent's or actor's phone number), the character the actor is auditioning for, and space for comments on each performance. I also have for each actor my own private index card with all vital information and my personal comments. He is also in my computer.

A day's audition session can last up to seven hours. Each actor is summoned from the waiting room, stage-door area, outer lobby, or wherever he or she is waiting. One by one each has about five to ten minutes to read. Some will be stopped by the end of the first page; others will be allowed to read through the complete set of audition sides, which could be from one to several pages. Some actors are immediately rejected, and others are put on the callback pile. Decisions are made throughout the following days and weeks, and callbacks are finally set up.

Creative Visualization Exercise:
AUDITIONING IN AN OFFICE

Prepare for creative visualization. See yourself in an agent's or casting director's office, whether or not you've been in one. Imagine what it would look like. Use a familiar office that very well could be used by an agent or casting director. See yourself sitting down to talk for a moment or getting right to the audition. You were instructed to bring in a monologue. Naturally, you have selected the perfect monologue to perform. You do this successfully and the agent shows much enthusiasm for your performance. Actually do the entire monologue in the exercise (in your head) and you are brilliant! Then you're asked to do a cold reading. (Choose the play you want to audition for). The agent or casting director gives you the sides, allowing you to take fifteen minutes to prepare. Visualize yourself doing this cold reading and performing with power, honesty, and humor. You are asked to leave ten pictures and resumés with the promise that you will be contacted within a day or so regarding an audition for a major production. You chat for a while, talking about your goals and dreams. The agent or casting director expresses excitement over you. Hear what the person is saying. You get ready to leave. You float out of the office.

THE AUDITION IS SERIOUS BUSINESS

This is not a social event; therefore, do not socialize! Stick to the reason why you are there—to prepare for your audition.

I suggest that you face the wall, preferably in a corner to avoid eye contact with others in the room, and prepare with your back to everyone. Stay far enough away from the noise but close enough to hear your name or number being called.

I know a young actor who goes to auditions and has a grand time goofing around with his fellow actors, displaying for them an outgoing, jovial personality, creating hilarity and laughter in the waiting room. His behavior once prompted a director to remark that he couldn't wait to see all the personality in the performance, but when the actor entered the audition studio and began his reading, it didn't take long to discover that he checked that marvelous personality at the door and brought in only the actor, leaving the person outside. His performance was wooden.

Don't expend energy in the wrong place with the wrong people! Of course, as serious as the audition process should be for you, you should be enjoying it.

Treat your audition appointments as a business. There is a job opening and you are applying for it. You need the job and the experience of working before a live audience or in front of a camera. Each audition, whether it ends in rejection or acceptance, is a valuable learning experience that brings you closer to the day when you can support yourself through your acting and once and for all dump your job as a waiter or word processor. You need the credit on your resumé, the contacts, the exposure, and the money!

You will be doing either a monologue or a cold reading. The casting notice in the trade paper or on your union call-board will run a character breakdown that advises the actor which is preferred, or your agent or manager will tell you. Occasionally you will be asked to do an improvisation. This means that you will be told of an interesting plot that might involve a couple of characters; you will be asked to act it out in your own words with no time to prepare. The director wants to see if you can think under pressure and still be creative. You might be asked to recall a very sad or happy story from your life and tell it to the auditors. One director I worked with had the actors audition this way, and at least ten actors that day had every person in the theater reduced to heart-wrenching sobs and tears! Once a director stopped an actor in the middle of his cold-reading audition and instructed him to do the rest of the reading as Columbo from the television series. The actor grabbed a raincoat someone had draped over a seat, put it on, and with his fountain pen as cigar, continued his reading outdoing Peter Falk. We were all doubled over with laughter. He got the part.

When an agent shows enough interest in you to want to see your work, you will be performing a monologue or two for him. He will determine if he wants to represent you from this performance, his interview with you, your past experience, and your appearance.

To determine whether or not to have you audition for a production, casting directors might also request a monologue, but probably will give you copy (sides from a television commercial) or sides from the production currently being cast by his office.

Theater directors will probably have you do a cold reading from the play you will be auditioning for, but many want you to bring a monologue to them first. If they like what they see, you will do the cold reading at the callback.

When doing a cold reading, you don't have to announce who you are and what you will be doing. You've been announced by the monitor and we know which character you are auditioning for because it is written on our daily audition schedules. However, at times the organization is sloppy and they won't know who you are auditioning for. In that case they will ask you when you come before them.

THE DAY OF YOUR AUDITION

Wear what you feel the character you are auditioning for could possibly wear, according to your knowledge of this person. The character breakdown in the actor's trade papers supplies you with information about the character. Or your agent, manager, casting director, or producer's office can tell you something about the character. Don't be timid about placing phone calls to these people to ask questions. Wear what evokes for you the feeling of the character.

Women should not wear slacks or jeans unless it is strongly indicated that the character lives in them. By and large your most tasteful daytime outfit is the best thing to wear. But do think about the cultural and economic background of the character.

Men should wear slacks, not jeans, and a jacket. Don't go overboard. If you are auditioning for *Dracula* there is no need to wear a cape, but you should wear a dark suit.

At the risk of sounding sexist, I advise women, "If you've got it, flaunt it!" Like chicken soup, it wouldn't hurt. Show those shapely legs off with a miniskirt. Display that tiny waist. However, please do not show up looking like a walking ad for a girlie magazine. I also advise men to do the same if they are endowed with a muscular frame. Of course, a jacket will cover the muscles, so perhaps you might want to remove it at the conclusion of your reading. It is possible that your character doesn't wear a jacket. If that's the case remove it when you are preparing offstage and carry it in.

PROPER BEHAVIOR BEFORE
THE AUDITION

Please do not be rude to the monitor, as this person not only represents the production but has been instructed by the director to reveal any behavioral problems an actor displays. I have been witness to several instances when an actor gave a marvelous performance that was worthy of a callback but his or her name was removed from the callback list because of reported bad behavior or attitude in the waiting room. The director wants to start off with as much harmony as possible, and an actor with an attitude doesn't create positive visions.

COURTEOUS BEHAVIOR TO
THE AUDITORS

Obviously, a good attitude is also expected in front of the auditors, but unbelievable as it sounds, many actors have displayed rude behavior.

We were auditioning actors for a new Broadway musical, and the auditions were being held on the stage of a Broadway theater. An actress who had passed her singing audition a few days earlier was now going to do her reading. Before she began, she announced to the director that she was going to do it with a southern accent. The director, a highly successful and much loved and respected man, replied that he did not want the part done with a southern accent. This should have been the end of the discussion, but she insisted that she saw the character that way. The director repeated that he did not see it that way. She replied that she had rehearsed it with a southern accent (she had access to the entire script a few days in advance because she was an up-and-coming star). He repeated his objection once more. She huffed and gave in, but not before she reiterated that she really thought the character should be southern. We could not believe her audacity and, of course, there was no way that she was going to be hired no matter how good her reading was.

On another occasion, an actor was ushered onto the stage of an off-Broadway theater to audition for the lead in a new play. Because he too was a star on the rise, he had been given the entire script to read in advance. When introduced to the playwright sitting next to me, the actor said to him, "How do you do? Boy, your script really needs a lot of work." The playwright wanted him ejected from the theater right then and had no interest in listening to the reading. By the way, the play ran for three years and was nominated for an Obie, the off-Broadway award for the best play of the year. The actor who got the part went on to Broadway to star in a major musical and win a Tony Award for best actor.

Another time, an actor not only insulted the auditors

but gave a bad reading as well. Later that day, I received a frantic phone call from his agent, apologizing for his client's behavior. She told me that he had received news that his mother had died right before he left for his audition, and he was in shock and was not responsible for his conduct. She begged me to allow him to come back and read again. I conferred with my director and playwright and when I repeated what she had told me, they agreed to give him another chance (but not until his mother was buried!). He read again the following week and he got the part.

I could tell many stories about bad behavior, but I think you get my "drift."

I also believe it is proper to thank your reader at the conclusion of your audition and thank your auditor, as well.

Creative Visualization Exercise: PROPER AND COURTEOUS BEHAVIOR

Prepare for the exercise. Visualize yourself checking in with the monitor. He or she is brisk with you, on the brink of being downright rude. Come through with calm behavior and perhaps even with humor. Suppose the monitor tells you that you will have to wait for almost an hour before you can be seen. On top of this delay, the sides will not be available to you until about five minutes before your audition. This should upset you, and rightly so. How do you handle it? After all, what can you do? You can complain, but your complaint will be interpreted as an "attitude." So grin and bear it. Visualize yourself in this situation or one that is seemingly unfair to you. Handle it. If, indeed, you receive the sides five minutes before your audition, you will be doing an ice-cold reading. This kind of audition will be covered in this book. Just remember: If there is a problem, there is a solution.

Visualize yourself before the auditors. You had been given the entire script to read in advance of your audition.

You feel that the script has problems that perhaps are fixable, and if they are fixed this could be a very interesting play or film. You are introduced to the writer. Obviously, a "How do you do?" is appropriate. What else, if anything, will you say to the writer? Choose something and say it. Find something positive to say without compromising your integrity. Surely you can come up with something positive about the script. Continue with courtesy and do your reading magnificently. Continue to put yourself in adverse situations, and come through like a professional with class in every instance.

THE PERSON READING
WITH YOU

Do not choose to read with another actor. A reader is provided for the auditions. This person is a member of the production staff or an actor hired by the day at AEA or SAG minimal wage. The union rule states that an actor must read with a reader, not another actor who is auditioning for the same play, even if that actor is auditioning for another part. It would appear that there would be no competition or conflict if you read with another actor, but let me assure you this is not the case. There is another actor up there with you who wants to be noticed; his or her determination could result in some very strange and inappropriate behavior on the audition stage that might interfere with your reading. You must not allow anyone to upstage you under these circumstances. You should be prepared for variables and conquer them with your strong choices and commitment to fulfill them.

The audition stage belongs to you, but the rule is broken all the time. Who is going to tell AEA or SAG? If no union representative is present at the audition, they don't know that an infraction is taking place. Actors are afraid to report violations because they don't want the producer to think of them as troublemakers. Some auditors are more interested in saving time and money than servicing the actors properly. The results of this practice can be devastating, as the following real-life example will demonstrate.

One day during the auditions for an off-Broadway play, the stage manager approached the director, who was seated at my side, and said an actress and actor who were waiting requested to read together. Each was reading the same scene. The director replied in the affirmative, stating we could save a few minutes. It was not hostility that motivated the director; it was stupidity! I often find, however, that it is difficult to tell them apart. And what started out as stupidity turned into hostility during and after the audition.

Several minutes later both the actors were ushered down the aisle and onto the stage, and they began their readings. The reader took a break and sat down to watch. Before they reached the end of the first page, the actor decided to playfully smack the actress on her behind. Mind you, there was no stage direction for this action, and in fact this character would never in his wildest dreams do such a thing to the female character; this was a woman the male character had just met! It was a poor choice for him to have made. When he executed the slap, the actress was caught off guard and she broke character. They had not planned the slap while they were preparing in the outer lobby.

By the time they got to the bottom of page two, he decided to kiss her passionately on the lips. In doing so, he swung her backwards, exposing her underwear to the entire house. Her handbag flew open, its contents spilling all over the stage. Her audition sides dropped from her hands, the pages scattering in all directions because she had removed the staple that held them together. When he released her, once again she was completely out of character and she was obviously mortified. I whispered to the director to stop this fiasco, but she replied that she was having the time of her life watching an actress squirm and an actor making an ass of himself!

When the reading was over, the young man made his exit as proud as could be and has not been seen since in the theater world. The young woman ran into the wings with tears flowing down her face. I went to her. I am responsible for the presence of all the actors at the audition, so when one is guilty of behaving like a horse's ass, my reputation suffers. At the same time, when an actor is assaulted in any way, "Mother Courage" here is up and at that actor's side in no time flat. I had seen the actress's work and was impressed, which is why I called her to audition, but on this day she erred in three ways.

The first mistake: She should have known that the reader is the best person for the job, not another actor also auditioning.

The second mistake: She didn't "use it" when he did those things to her.

The third mistake: She removed the staple from the sides. When they fell and each page went flying, she had to scramble about the stage to retrieve them.

Actors like to complain that the reader gives nothing to the actor and there is no one and nothing to play off, but never forget: The audition is not ensemble work.

When you know how to prepare for and perform at your audition, you do not want *anything* from the person reading with you! You must make your choices for yourself and the other character. You must play off what you have chosen for the other character, not play off the person doing the reading. No reader is going to give you what you want unless you audition every day of the year and perhaps stumble across one who will come through for you. If this ever happens, you will be aware of it instantly. Then you can play off the actor and enjoy the relationship. Sometimes the other actor will have made stronger and more interesting choices than you did; you will definitely feel it during the reading, so play off him and let him guide you through. But by and large do not expect anything from the other person. What he or she might be doing will be intrusive to your reading. It might appear to you that you are both in separate plays because of such a tremendous gap in acting styles and sensibilities, but don't worry. We, the auditors, know the play or film script and we will understand what you are doing if you continue along your own pathway. If the other actor is giving something way out of the ballpark or nothing at all, we will be grateful to you that you are providing an honest life up there. Make choices for both characters, and when the reader gives you nothing, you should be responding with your lines *as if* he gave you exactly what you expected. You don't want others to sabotage your audition, and they can't if you don't allow them to!

The panicked actress should have been able to stay in character and react as character to what the actor did. It was she, the actress, who got flustered, not the character. I have no objection to the actress being flustered as long as she then shares it with her character. The character might have gotten flustered too, though it would have been a poor choice for her to have been surprised into silence, as this actress was. The dialogue has to keep flowing and the script written by the writer must be serviced.

If you object strongly to something the actor or reader has done, give your true feelings to your character. For instance, if the reader doesn't speak up or turns from you or is not concentrating on you enough, allow yourself as character to be annoyed with him just as you, the actor, are. Your inner dialogue should be, "Look at him! He will hardly look at me and seems to be uninterested in me." Add this to your performance and try to get him to speak up and look at you.

Regarding the staple, had she left it in place, the pages would have fallen with a thud at her feet and they would have been back in her hands in a second.

If the auditor pairs you with another actor auditioning for the same play, you have the option to protest if it is a union production (and risk being thought of as a troublemaker), or to just go ahead and do your reading.

The two actors whose audition was a disaster had met each other for the first time in the outer lobby and talked to each other instead of each working on their sides alone. It was his idea to audition together, and she agreed. He did not tell her of his plans to slap and kiss her, though perhaps he thought of it during the reading.

His mistake, aside from reading with another actor,

was that he directed the reading when he should have been creating. Creating is internal and is the actor's job. The actor creates choices when he visualizes the history, background, and future of the character. Directing is peripheral and is the director's job. It involves staging and simply has no place in a cold-reading audition.

With direction comes physicalizing (physical movement by the actors). This is part of the rehearsal process, not the audition process. It is best to stay in place and not physicalize at the cold-reading audition. It is a reading, not a rehearsal or finished scene. Do not move about because *you do not know how* to move about in a cold reading! Movement will emerge during rehearsals when you are developing character. In the audition, use your body as a prop. It's the best prop you'll ever have! Stamp your foot, tremble, shake your head, turn away and turn back swiftly, and so forth.

One more word concerning the luckless auditioning couple. When I was in the wings with the actress, both comforting and scolding her, I told her I would ask the director, a woman who had won a Tony Award for her Broadway performance years before and who took pride in being a militant feminist, to give her another chance and allow her to read with the reader. This was the director's reply: "Hell, no! She had her chance and she blew it!" So much for sisterhood.

Creative Visualization Exercise:
BEING BRILLIANT DESPITE THE INFERIOR READER

Prepare for creative visualization. See yourself at a cold reading and put yourself in the situation where the reader is being physical toward you and acting in a most inappropriate manner. Keep your cool. Stay in character. Visualize yourself taking charge of the situation and turning the audition into a plus for you and an embarrassment for him. (Don't worry, he deserves it.) Use everything he does. Allow it all to happen to your character. If things get out of hand and he goes overboard, you have the option to ad-lib and tell him to cease his inappropriate behavior. You emerge victoriously, knowing that you conducted yourself professionally and with dignity—and you didn't allow the reader to sabotage your reading.

DURING THE READING

Use both hands to hold your audition sides. This reminds us that it is a cold-reading audition, not a rehearsed scene. Do not memorize. Read.

You should focus your eyes on three places throughout the reading. The first, of course, is the page; the second, the other person; the third is the fourth wall, which is the space in front of you (downstage) and over the heads of the audience. Most actors never use this wall during their cold-reading auditions—and what a mistake not to! Those who do give more of themselves to the audience, therefore achieving a stronger stage presence.

Do not look down at the floor. We don't want to see your eyelids. We want to see your eyes. Don't cut us off.

Do not give us a profile reading. We want to see two eyes, not one! Eyes are what people focus on when someone is talking. Face forward, and when you look at the other person, turn your neck and head to him but not your body. Think of the audience too as the other person. In a manner of speaking we are. We very often identify with the listener, not the talker. After all, we spend the entire time in our seats listening. We are hearing the dialogue for the first time, just as your character is.

There is no need to gesticulate heavily during the reading. You may take one hand off the pages momentarily to gesture or to mime taking a drink and then letting go of the glass (just let it drop), but by and large, keep those hands on the pages. You may also reach out and gently touch the reader if you so desire.

Use your left thumb to guide your eye down the page so that at pivotal moments you are able to lift your eyes to look at the other person and at the fourth wall. You can look out there while you are listening to the person. Keep your thumb at your next line and take a sneak peek at the other person's last three words so that at that moment, you can return your eyes to the page and to your line. Listen to the other person's dialogue; don't read it. If the reader has only one line of dialogue, you don't have that much time to look forward (downstage) as you would if the reader had several lines. There is no need to stare at him during his dialogue. Look forward and above the auditors' heads. We are also listening as you are, so let's listen together. The worst thing to behold on an audition stage is the actor whose head is buried in the pages.

With your right hand, keep your thumb under each page on the lower right corner. Each time you turn a page, get that thumb on to the next page immediately. You will be ready to effortlessly turn each page without breaking the verbal rhythm.

Stand up as straight as you can (unless it is strongly indicated in the stage directions that your character always slouches). There are two ways to stand. One is when you seem to press your rib cage into your stomach, creating a slouch; your feet actually look as if they are embedded into the floor. It appears that the actor is trying to hide from us and is very uncomfortable being there. The actor's stage presence is weak and unattractive. The astute auditor picks up on this immediately. The other, preferable way to stand is so that a bolt of energy appears to be rising through you from the bottom of your feet, up through your legs and torso, to the top of your head. Stand tall with your body reflecting a sense of importance and immediacy. Put your weight equally on both feet and lean slightly forward and very much upward! Don't forget: Today is the most important day of your (character's *and* actor's) life, and the person to whom you are talking is the most important person in your life.

Confront the other person at all times. Do not turn your body away so that your back is to him while you are listening or talking for more than a beat or two. You will be alienating yourself from him, therefore from your auditors. Actors tend to turn away at a point in the reading when their characters are abashed, offended, insulted, outraged, resentful, piqued, hurt, or in a huff. These are the times when you *must* strongly confront the other person and communicate your feelings directly to him instead of away from him. You are cheating yourself by not playing off such a strong emotion, head-on. This kind of staging is television and the old Hollywood blocking so that both faces can be seen fully in one frame. It is a device you should always avoid. In life many of us might turn away in the midst of these kinds of emotions and look away from the person who brought them on, but the truth of life does not translate well to the truth of theater. Even if you are auditioning for television, do not take it upon yourself to block and play it this way. Do as you would in a theater audition. We must see strong communication and relationship for the entire reading for television, film, and theater auditions. There is no difference as far as we are concerned.

When you are auditioning with an actor who is auditioning for the other character in the scene, the following problem may arise. He or she is not standing stage center, which is clearly the best spot for both of you. Perhaps the actor is upstage (farther away from the audience) or all the way right or left, but you want to stay stage center and you wish the actor was closer to you. You don't want to hurt your own performance by turning toward the actor and displaying the back of your head, but you don't want to go upstage because you feel it is too far from the auditors or there is not enough light there. The way to handle and correct this situation is to first be aware as character that he or she doesn't seem to want to be near you. Then remember that because today is the most important day in your life and the other character is the most important person in your life, you must get the actor to come closer to you. Your inner dialogue should be, "He doesn't even want to be near me. This is very hurtful to me." Give any displeasures or frustrations you might have toward the actor reading with you to your character. I don't care what the situation is on the page. You can add this to any one. The next thing to do is this: Approach the actor and on *your* dialogue, not his, gently link your arm through his and walk him, as you are talking, to center stage or the hot spot (where the light is brightest onstage). He *will* follow your lead and allow you to guide him, but this must be done during your dialogue. Then you are not intruding on him as you would be if he were doing the talking.

You are not required to be physically involved with the other actor or the reader in a cold reading. If the stage directions say that you passionately kiss, don't do it during the first audition (especially with a reader). Romantic and sexual passion evolves through character development and must also be staged. However, you must indicate that you have no aversions to being touched or kissed. When we see an actor cringe and recoil from a somewhat benign type of physicality at the audition, we worry that there might be intimacy problems with that actor and will not consider a callback no matter how good the reading was.

I remember an actress who recoiled when the other actor reached over to touch her and kiss her on her cheek. She almost jumped out of her skin and later remarked that she loathed being touched! Naturally she could not be taken seriously for the part.

Do not brutalize your partner. No pushing, shoving, hitting, punching, pinching, or kicking. When auditors see a physically aggressive actor at the reading, we sincerely become frightened of that actor. He is sent on his way. A superb reading will not save him. We feel it is totally inappropriate conduct and want none of it. Physicalize by stamping your feet, taking a step back, forward, or sideways, or by smacking your own head. Remember, your body is your best prop. Use it.

STARTING A READING A SECOND TIME

During your reading, you might suddenly feel that it is not going well and you would like to start over again.

Please do not ask to start again. It's better to make a change midstream. As soon as you realize you would like to do your reading differently and better—simply start doing it! If you ask to start again, you are giving the auditor the opportunity to say, "Oh, that's okay, no need to do that. What you've done is fine. Thank you very much. Good-bye."

Be aware that if *you* know you are doing a bad reading, your auditors are also aware of it. Once they've seen work not to their liking, they would just as soon send you on your way and proceed to the next actor. The auditors will be impressed if you simply change your performance. Their attitude will be, "Good for him! He knew he was going down the toilet and he saved himself. Now I like what he's doing."

Directors will be thrilled to see that you are so aware and that you can "self-correct." They will be gratified to see that they won't have to spoon-feed you. That means that they won't have to tell you everything. You will be able to tell yourself and fix problems without constantly depending on your director.

NO PINTER PAUSES

There should be no dead spots in between your dialogue with the other person. Harold Pinter, the brilliant playwright, screenwriter, and director, actually writes pauses into his scripts between each character's dialogue. But for you to take time before responding to the other character's dialogue, even if only for a few beats, can slow down your reading and make it seem as if it is being dragged out of you. In a cold reading you are not ready for a Pinter

Pause. It becomes a dead spot as we wait for your next line while absolutely nothing happens during the silence. You can't justify the silence yet because you haven't developed character, read and analyzed the script, or rehearsed it.

What you must do is listen to what the other character is saying, deal with the words *as* he is saying them, and respond instantly. Do not wait a few beats before responding. Keep the action going (not at a galloping pace) so that it flows. During your dialogue, do not rush—make it very conversational.

Another reason not to do a Pinter Pause is that you are inviting an auditor to say, "Thank you. That will be enough." He doesn't feel uncomfortable about stopping you because he wasn't interrupting you. No one was saying anything! He got you during a Pinter Pause.

YOUR CHOICES ARE PRIVATE

Do not reveal to *anyone*—reader, actor, casting director, director, producer, playwright, stage manager, monitor—what your choices are for the character you are auditioning for! These people do not understand the actor's process. If you divulge your inner life choices, the playwright or director will most likely say, "That's not what my character is about. She's not in love with the other character as this actor has chosen to be. She obviously doesn't understand my play." You will be out! They don't realize that in order for you to get to the place you want to get to, you must take a circuitous route. I told you they are result-oriented. Keep your choices to yourself and give them the result they want—your way.

GIVE BACK CLEAN SIDES

Before you hand back your sides, erase any markings you made on them. The monitor will relay to the director and producer that you wrote all over them and they will resent you for doing that to their precious property. Most monitors relish reporting any infraction. This is their way of demonstrating to their superiors how great their allegiance to the production is. A monitor is the low man on the totem pole and aspires to greater heights in production. Monitors will do whatever they have to do to look good and please the director and producer.

Creative Visualization Exercise: A SUCCESSFUL AUDITION

Prepare for the exercise. Visualize yourself on a stage standing near the stage manager who will read with you. The auditors are before you in the third row. You have done your preparation and have your choices in your head. You're holding the sides with your left thumb ready to glide down as the dialogue progresses. You've got your right thumb under the page on the lower right corner ready to instantly turn the page when required. You begin the reading. You lift your eyes from the page and turn your head to look at the other person at pivotal moments. You listen by using the fourth wall, and you are even looking up during your own dialogue for a beat or two. You are standing tall and you feel secure and powerful on the stage because it is there for you and only you during this time. You confront the other person at all times and do not turn from him at an emotional moment, but you turn your head to him during the highlights of the emotions. When he walks away from you at one point and does not return, you go to him, and during your dialogue, you gently link arms with him and walk him back to center stage. You are not afraid to reach out and gently touch him at a point in your reading. You feel that perhaps you are "going off" at one point so you just put yourself right back on the track again, changing what you are doing and making it better! You can feel that your performance has gotten stronger now. You are responding to the other person's dialogue immediately. There are no dead spots. The audition comes to an end. You feel totally justified that you gave a powerful, appealing, and intelligent reading. You are thanked and you leave the stage feeling elated.

THE "I WOULD NEVER SAY THAT" ACTOR

When actors say, "I would never say that" or, "I would never handle the situation the way this character does; this just isn't me," my retort is, "Who asked you?"

Of course it's not you. Do you think playwrights and screenwriters write about me and you? As an actor, can you honestly say that you want to play just "you"? Acting is playing all kinds of characters who are indeed different from you. Each time you read for a character, you discover what it is like to step into their shoes. What you also must allow is for them to step into yours! Each character teaches you a new sense of humanity about yourself and others.

Acting is playing characters who say and do things that you would never say or do. If you say that you would never throw a writer's script into a burning stove or put a bullet to your head, then you will never be able to play *Hedda Gabler*. If you say that you would never murder anyone, then you could never be able to play *Macbeth*, or his lady. If you say you would never blind six horses, then you will never be able to play Alan in *Equus*. I daresay, you will be cutting yourself off from some of the most dynamic and important characters in dramatic literature.

Actors also love to say, "I would never be sent up for that part." The actor is the last person to decide what parts he will be sent up for, and the actor who makes such a statement is closing himself up in a small casting box. It should not be the concern of the actor what parts he will be allowed to read for. The objective of the actor is to go to any audition where they will let you read. Don't concern yourself with what "they" (the auditors) are looking for. Concentrate on presenting your acting strengths.

Find the character in you and interpret it your way and make very personal life-and-death choices. Let the auditors decide you are not right, but remember, you are not only auditioning for this production. You are also auditioning for future ones, and a casting director, director, playwright, and producer are out there watching you, offering you the opportunity to show *your* strengths. If they love your work but reject you for the current production, they might just say, "He's not for this but he's wonderful so let's keep him in the active file to have him back for something else." Or after seeing all the actors, they may say, "He didn't give us the character on the page but maybe the pages should be changed!"

The character of Gloria in the film *White Men Can't Jump* was supposed to be a Wasp, until Rosie Perez read for the role. Ron Shelton, the director, started to rethink the part because Ms. Perez gave such a surprising and honest reading. She got the part and Gloria was rewritten from an Ivy League college student to an "ex–disco queen" from Brooklyn.

Acting is not just playing characters similar to ourselves. Some you will approve of and like and some you will not. If the character says or does something that is totally at variance with your values—great! You will really be acting.

When you begin your preparation and immediately get into first-person character, you cannot disapprove of "yourself." You will be playing murderers, cheats, liars, deceivers, and callous, maniacal, diabolic, pretentious characters. Can you describe yourself as being imbued with any of these qualities? I hope not! Remember, there are opposites in every character, and once you are in first person, you will find the humanity and vulnerability.

If you put yourself in a neat little casting box that prohibits you from going beyond your own personality, you are steeped in limitations and you cannot think of yourself as an actor so you will not find success as one.

"I WANT HIM/HER TO ACCEPT ME THE WAY I AM"

I would say that these words are the ones most frequently spoken by actors on behalf of their characters during preparation for the audition. First of all, let's get rid of the word "accept" and replace it with the word, "love." Other worthless words are "understand," "acknowledge," "approve," and "admire." The bottom line is that your character is always fighting for love and through the love, acceptance, understanding, acknowledgment, approval, and admiration will follow.

When I ask an actor what he is fighting for from the other character and he answers he is fighting for understanding, I reply, "Okay, he understands you. Now, how is his understanding going to enhance the rest of your life?" You see, I can understand you and who you are and why you do and say the things you do, but where is the love? Understanding does not equal love, but love can engender understanding.

Make choices that will allow your character to grow and become a fuller person. It is much more interesting to say, "I'm not so crazy about myself the way I am. *I* don't love me the way I am. How can I expect him to? I want to change and I desperately need him to love me enough to be sensitive to my needs so that he can help me to change myself and my life."

LOVE: THE STRONGEST CHOICE OF ALL

Assume that all plays are about love, all kinds of love. We are familiar with romantic love (often selfish), familial love (mostly altruistic), and our love for our pets and friends. But what about recognizing and appreciating kind words and gestures made by an individual who is not an integral part of our life, but perhaps just a stranger who enters our life momentarily and performs a deed that enriches it?

For example, I was walking down the street, and I heard a voice behind me in the distance calling "Miss, Miss." I turned and about halfway down the block saw a man walking toward me whom I did not recognize, so I assumed he was calling to someone else. I continued to walk, and once again he called out, "Miss, wait a minute." I glanced back and he was walking faster. I looked about me to see who he was addressing, but no other woman was nearby. I picked up my pace and he yelled, "Miss, please wait a minute." I turned again and saw that he was waving something in his hand. I considered running across the street, but the traffic was heavy. He caught up with me, and I saw that he was clutching some cash in his hand. He said, "When you took your cash out of the bank machine down the block, I was across the street waiting for the light to change, and I noticed that when you put the cash in your back jeans pocket, it all came back out again when you took your hand out, and you didn't know it. I ran in between the traffic to get all the bills that were flying around, before someone stole them. I've been chasing you down the block and calling to you to stop so I could give you back your money. Boy, you sure are a fast walker."

What do you think I felt for him? That's right. Love. It was indeed a loving gesture made by a stranger whom I had no intentions of ever seeing again, but for that moment, I sure did have love in my heart for him. He fearlessly retrieved my $60, which I'd intended to spend on groceries, including that evening's dinner. I thanked him from the bottom of my heart and continued on my way to the supermarket with a terrific feeling. At the checkout counter, I had a resurgence of the loving feeling and realized that had it not been for his honesty, I would have been in a very uncomfortable situation at that moment when I reached for my money.

As I was preparing the dinner, I thought of him and felt a nice glow, and during dinner I shared the story with my companion and once more I had a special feeling.

This stranger brought a lot of love into my life that day and made me feel that perhaps there is a glimmer of hope for humanity, even in New York!

When Diane Keaton in *The Godfather II* told Al Pacino that she never would have thought that the day would come when she could now say that she didn't love him anymore, she said it *with* love. A lesser actress would have left out the love; after all, she no longer loved him. But Ms. Keaton dealt with the absence of love and the sadness over the loss. If he were to become the man he once was, perhaps she could love him again. At least this was a possible and certainly an intelligent choice for the actress to make.

Always deal with love as both word and emotion in making choices for your character.

SELF-INDULGENCE

The audience has the luxury of being self-indulgent. Self-indulgence has no place in the life of an actor during a performance. The audience member can indulge, entertain, and pamper himself in self-pity, tears, laughter, and all sentiments and enthusiasms. The actor is *acting* and must maintain a strong discipline and not allow identification with the character to interfere with his performance. The actor must be in control. Self-indulgence at the cold-reading audition is death to the reading. I will explain.

An actor was in the middle of his reading. Suddenly he

began to breathe in short sporadic spurts and his body began to tremble. His words were delivered as cries and screams. Then he fell to the floor and crumbled into a fetal position. We sat in horror, frozen in our seats. Then I bolted from my chair, ran to him, got down on the floor, put my arms around him, and held and rocked him, telling him, "It's all right" continuously for about five minutes until he came out of it.

The scene he was reading dealt with a death, and the actor drew on his father's recent death. It became so painful that his personal loss took over and he was no longer the character in the play but himself mourning the death of his father.

A similar situation occurred with an actress who threw her sides to the floor and ran screaming into the ladies' room, locking herself in a stall. There she stayed for over ten minutes, reduced to wall-shattering sobs. She had drawn on a recent real-life situation; she had caught her husband cheating on her and he left her for the other woman.

Do not draw on and incorporate an unresolved emotional trauma from your life. Nothing is worth putting yourself through such a devastating experience.

There is a second, less emotional response that is also death to the reading. Because it is so painful to draw on a recent trauma, the actor pushes the experience completely away, therefore rendering a characterless and languid reading. Of course, the actor is only protecting him- or herself, but the proper way to protect yourself is to wait until your trauma is resolved and you can handle it —and use it effectively.

It is a different situation when rehearsing for a monologue audition or during a rehearsal on a production. If you draw on an unresolved trauma for your monologue rehearsal, you will know soon enough whether or not you can handle the trauma. If you cry, you are alone and not exposing yourself and your still open wounds to the public. You have to work it out. Either you will decide that you can use your past loss even if the initial try resulted in tears, or you will discard your choice and substitute another one. It may be that the nature of the material is inappropriate for you at the present time.

Another form of self-indulgence is when the actor does his homework in front of us. This means that he did not assimilate his or her choices for the character properly during the preparation. The actor might not have even prepared at all, and what we watch is not so much of a reading and a performance as a preparation. This is deadly to watch because the pacing is slowed to almost a halt. The actor and the reading are dull and unprofessional.

Do not be a self-indulger regarding your talents. A seriously dedicated actor never knows that he or she is brilliant. There is perpetual self-doubt and concern. The actor who emerges triumphantly through his or her magnetic influence, stunning presence, intense emotionalism, and perceptive intelligence, filling theaters with ticket buyers, sums up the achievement by stating, "It felt good."

Artists do as they can. It is the audience and professional critics who bestow praise upon them. They proceed through their theatrical careers plagued by uncertainty, hoping they can service the next production well.

As an actor striving to learn everything that will bring you to audiences, you must forge ahead with vigor and belief that yours will and must be the preeminent performance at the audition. Do as you can. Make it feel good.

LIFE-AND-DEATH CHOICES FOR AN OPENING NIGHT PERFORMANCE AT THE COLD-READING AUDITION

For each audition I want you to fight like hell with the strongest life-and-death choices you can possibly make. The following illustrates just how hard the fight should be.

Many years ago on the lower east side of Manhattan, there was a famous theater company called The Group Theatre. Its members were stage luminaries of the day and included future leaders in the theater world, such as Stella Adler, Harold Clurman, Lee Strasberg, Sanford Meisner, Bobby Lewis, and many others.

For one production, they hired a young man named Muni Weisenfreund, later known in Hollywood as Paul Muni, as an understudy. In this play, at the end of Act One, the landlord enters the apartment of a destitute family unable to pay the rent. The landlord confronts the husband and tells him that he and his family must vacate the apartment. Another family wants it and can pay for it. The husband begs him to allow them to stay. He pleads and asks the landlord where they will go. He has no job and cannot secure one because no work is available. He has no money and it is the middle of the winter. His children will freeze and starve to death. The landlord does not bend. He demands that they vacate immediately. The last line in the act is spoken by the landlord. He says, "You will leave this apartment." He storms off, leaving the husband standing helpless with his arms stretched up to heaven.

Mr. Muni understudied the husband, and one night he got to go on. During that scene, he proceeded to beg and plead, not changing one word, and when the landlord opened his mouth to deliver the last line in the act, he was heard to say, "All right! You can stay!" and stormed off into the wings.

The curtain came down and there was quite a commotion backstage. The actor was asked why he didn't deliver the proper line, and his response was, "I couldn't say no to him!"

Do no less than Mr. Muni did. By the way, when the second-act curtain went up, the landlord reappeared in the apartment and said, "I changed my mind. You must leave this apartment." The play was resumed as it was written.

Mr. Muni went on to be a Hollywood star. Nobody can remember the name of the actor he understudied.

. . .

After you've been hired, your director works with you in the rehearsal process for a couple of weeks for film and for four weeks or longer for theater on the development of your character, script interpretation, relationships, conflicts, and blocking. For the audition, the objective is to discover an extraordinary and finished performance despite the fact that you were given only three or four pages from the script minutes before, that you have no knowledge of the play or screenplay, and that there has been no direction, ensemble work, or rehearsals.

Does the director really want and expect you to give an opening night performance under such circumstances? On one hand, yes! On the other hand, of course not. Well, you ask, what is *that* supposed to mean?

First of all, how does anyone *know* what an opening night performance should be like in preproduction? Even the person who wrote the script can't really know. Of course, concepts, visions, dreams, and imagery are in the heads of the writer, director, and some casting directors.

During the audition and rehearsal process, many of the concepts are metamorphosed, visions are shattered and re-created, dreams are revised, and imagery is transformed. If you are bold, forthright, and unreserved in the choices you make for your character, if you dare to expose your vulnerabilities, warts and all, if you respond to the absurdities and ironies all around you in life and on the pages, if you have a very special inner ear and eye that, like antennae, pick up on nuances, if you have some awareness and a lot of curiosity about human behavior patterns, you just might be a candidate for getting callbacks, succeeding at them, and being hired. Craft alone cannot enable an actor to affect an audience. You must give the words a validity and not be less than what is written.

Your audition performance should be as appealing, powerful, and profound as an opening night performance. The choices you make for your character during your preparation don't have to be the same as the playwright's;

indeed, you probably won't know what the playwright's or screenwriter's choices are anyway, but yours must be as strong and powerful as his.

The following story illustrates what I mean. After being hired as casting director on a play, I was instructed by the playwright not to allow anyone access to his script without his permission. The sides, of course, would be made available to actors with audition appointments. Naturally, I complied with his wishes.

One day after an actress had completed an excellent audition, the playwright turned to me and said, "I thought I told you not to let anyone read my play!" I told him that I hadn't. "That's impossible," he replied. "She had to read it. She knows everything about the entire play!"

The actress was given a callback and ended up getting the part, and rightly so. Early in rehearsals, she and I were talking, and she confided to me that she couldn't believe it when she got the callback and then the part because when she finally read the entire play *after* her callback, she discovered that the choices she had made for her character had *nothing* to do with *anything* going on in the play!

She got the part because she made life-and-death choices, making the stakes as high as she could with powerful needs and feelings for the other character in the scene. She did not concern herself with what might have been happening in the pages *not* given to her. She created an interesting history and background for her character, made the present momentous, and fought with all her being for her future.

Working off the highlights on three pages, she was able to service the playwright's play and also create a play within the play consisting of her private choices. These were not the same as the playwright's, but they were as important and intense.

Think of the sides presented to you as the entire play (or screenplay). A beginning, a middle, and an end are on those few pages. Assume at all times that the play deals with life-and-death situations so that your choices—and therefore your performance—will be as strong or even stronger than the playwright's choices.

At the audition, don't give us a rehearsal performance. Much more of you is required. Your rehearsal performances are for practice and growth prior to a public presentation. Consider the audition a public presentation. The auditors are your first audience. Remember, most directors, playwrights, and some casting directors are frustrated actors! So make us green with envy over your reading. Make us wish that we could do what you've just done.

When you are finished with your reading, don't break character immediately. In fact, if you are deeply involved as character in the event and relationship, it should be difficult for you to immediately break character. Give yourself a count of five to "let the curtain fall." At this time, you will be thanked and sent on your way. Perhaps the auditor will ask you about your availability regarding callbacks and production dates. Of course, if you are asked such questions, this could indicate that he loved your performance. Perhaps so, but assume nothing!

Years ago, I auditioned for a Broadway musical. I sang my song on the stage for the composer, lyricist, and director, sitting in the third row. After I finished, they asked me all about myself and my availability regarding callbacks. We spoke and joked back and forth for no less than ten minutes. I had a grand time and just knew I was a shoe-in! I never heard from them again.

Creative Visualization Exercise:
LIFE-AND-DEATH CHOICES

Prepare for the exercise. Choose a character from a play or film and prepare to audition for that part. Make the strongest life-and-death choices you can make about what you desperately must have from the other character. Personalize and substitute, bringing the character as close to you as possible. Fight like hell! Visualize all this. No barriers. Go over the top. Don't be afraid of being too big. Be honest.

INFERIOR MATERIAL

Sometimes sides are presented to you, and as you read the pages, you discover that the material is third-rate garbage. Under these conditions, you'd better make more interesting and stronger choices than the writer's or you will be allowing him to sabotage your audition. By the way, "inferior" scripts can be turned into masterpieces with rewriting done during the previews right up to the opening night. And film scripts can turn brilliant during the shooting.

Perhaps you find the writing inferior, but thematically it is highly appealing to you. Or you admire the writing but object to the theme. Or perhaps you feel that the script is commendable but you dislike your character.

You will not be able to give a brilliant performance at the reading unless you find something redeeming on those pages. Concentrate on what you *do* like. When you are told that you got the part, you can always decline if the material is so objectionable that you would be hard pressed to discover redeeming qualities somewhere in the script.

STAGE DIRECTIONS

Stage directions are meant for the actual production, not for the audition; therefore, read them and discard them. The only reason to read them during your preparation is to acquire insight into your character; however, this will rarely occur. Incorporate some of them minimally into your reading, but not at the risk of interrupting your verbal rhythm. We *know* you can open a door, close a window, light a cigarette, pour a drink, make a bed, or set a table. What we don't know about you is if you can openly and interestingly communicate in words and be involved believably in a relationship onstage that extends beyond, to the audience or camera. Show us that you can.

Do not take it upon yourself to write your own stage directions. Chances are your choices will be at variance with what the playwright had in mind or with the director's concept. I recall an actress who once took a banana out of her handbag during her reading, peeled it, and ate it throughout the remainder of her reading. The character she was reading for, a young Jackie Kennedy–type, would never do such a thing.

You certainly don't want to antagonize the director by showing not only that you want to act in the production but that you want to direct it too. The director will be cautious and worried that you might not want to allow him or her to be the one and only director. Wait until you get the part. Then you can invent and share your concepts with the director.

Don't fall into the trap of following passive stage directions that describe your character as being bored or not listening to the other character. You don't know *how* to play "emotionally inactive" in a cold reading! It takes a number of rehearsals to learn how to be effectively, actively, and interestingly bored! In a cold reading, have your character not wanting to be bored and fighting against it.

If you have a word of dialogue buried in between a lot of stage directions, you could miss it completely during the audition, so during the preparation, underline the word with a pencil to make it visible during the reading.

Don't ignore the other character's dialogue, as some actors are prone to do. Plays are written about relationships and conflicts between characters, and you *must* be aware of what the other character is saying to you. Each word of dialogue is a response to the other character's words. If you simply dismiss the other dialogue, you are cheating yourself out of the heart and soul of the relationship, the scene, and the play—and out of a callback.

PREPARATION VERSUS REHEARSAL

There is an enormous difference between preparation for the cold-reading audition and rehearsing a monologue. In a preparation, you only have a few pages of dialogue from the script to work with. There is no such thing as character development, script analysis and interpretation, ensemble work, or staging. You don't have to memorize lines, be directed, or work with props. There is no scene partner to prepare with. Therefore, because these elements constitute a rehearsal and none is at your disposal, what you are doing is preparing for your audition, not rehearsing.

In a cold-reading preparation and performance you have to do without the luxury of time to experiment or make mistakes and correct them. Nor are you able to analyze or intellectualize, which is just as well, because I consider this to be a waste of time and even detrimental for an actor. The time and effort you expend doing this will prevent you from dealing with visceral feelings, such as emotional needs, confrontation, desires, vulnerabilities, fears, anxieties, and desperation.

These emotional complexities within the characters should be dealt with by the actor, and there is nothing intellectual about them. Leave that to the critics on opening night.

AUDITIONING FOR A FAMILIAR PLAY

Perhaps you are familiar with the play because it is being revived and you saw it the first time, or you read it or saw the movie version. Beware! Don't be cocky and think that all is a piece of cake because you know the play. You know the play only from an audience member's point of view, not the actor's. Treat a familiar play as entirely new. Be prepared to play off only the pages given to you and forget the rest. When the actor incorporates events from other scenes, the action on those few pages dissipates. You may, of course, use what the playwright has given for your character's history and background, adding or substituting as you wish, but watch out for events that don't concern what is happening in the here and now, that is, on the pages given to you.

Knowledge of the play can contribute to the sabotaging of your reading when the relationship created by the playwright is not as strong as it should be for you.

As an example, let us turn to a play you may well be familiar with, Peter Shaffer's *Equus*. In one scene Dr. Dysart, a psychiatrist, is confiding in Hester. It is not stated in the audition sides who she is in relation to him, although one line indicates that she is not a nurse or doctor. Therefore, it is the actor's choice. Actually the *fact* of who she is is not important. It is their feelings toward one another that matter to us.

He is telling her how cheerless and monotonous his life and marriage is. He talks of how he has always done what has been expected of him. He admits that he hasn't kissed his wife in six years and that they take the same vacation year after year. He says that it is his fault that they've had no children because of his low sperm count, which he was too ashamed to reveal to his wife. He then talks of his patient, Alan, who blinded six horses, and as horrendous as the deed was, the doctor feels that Alan has at least reached out and committed an act of passion, something he, the doctor, has never done. It confuses him that Alan is called crazy and he is called sane.

Hester is shocked by his pronouncements and pleads for him to evaluate Alan's troubled behavior with more clarity. She reminds him that he is a brilliant and renowned doctor and doesn't go around blinding horses.

On the page, a distraught person appears to be confiding in another person with a sympathetic ear. Nothing indicates romance or love between them. Knowledge of the entire play confirms this, so of course actors familiar with the play don't create such a situation for their characters. What a mistake! As Dr. Dysart, you should have as your mystery and secret that you are madly in love with Hester and wish to make passionate love to her right now. You should be longing to act out the fantasies you've been having about running off with Hester and having a glorious life together. You should be fighting for her to love you and want you and to come into your life and save you.

As Hester, you should be overjoyed when he tells you that he hasn't kissed his wife in six years. This is a grand discovery because you are madly in love with him and had no idea that he had such a bland relationship with his wife, until now! You should also be upset for him because he is the one you love, as well as an esteemed doctor. He has revealed some mixed-up and perhaps dangerous notions about himself in relation to Alan, so you should be frightened that he may be going off the deep end. He could forfeit his position and you may lose him entirely. You may never have him as the lover you have been dreaming of since the day you first met him.

This is your play within the play. The opposites. The inner life choices. You will have created a stronger relationship than the one created by the playwright. He didn't give this to you, but an inner life of loving each other does not interfere with anything on the pages. It compliments what is already there. You have created romantic and sexual love and raised the stakes. Mr. Shaffer gives us plenty —but not enough for the audition!

THE SIGNATURE (FAMILIAR) PERFORMANCE

When you have seen the actor of stature who originated the part you are auditioning for, beware of a built-in trap that you alone create and fall into.

Actors say, "I saw Dustin (or Meryl) do the part and I don't want to copy him or her."

You do not look like Dustin Hoffman or Meryl Streep.

You do not sound like them. You do not act like them. You are not them! Have you no sense of your personal identification as person and actor? Are you that frightened that you will relinquish your strengths and be swallowed up by Mr. Hoffman or Ms. Streep?

Do not fear that you will present a clone of them. Do not ignore what they did. Remember it well and allow Mr. Hoffman and Ms. Streep (or whomever) to *direct* you to the level of intensity required for the character. You are not going to *do* him or her; you are going to *use* him or her. You will be doing it your way, with his or her guidance! Let them be your *directors*.

Creative Visualization Exercise: AUDITIONING FOR THE FAMILIAR PLAY

Who are your favorite actors? Which performance was the one that most affected you? I want you to audition for that part. Prepare for creative visualization. Put yourself in the audition for the part. You know how he or she performed it. Allow the actor who originated the part to guide you through the reading. You have a wonderful director to help you. Give the same level of intensity and passion. Communicate strongly as he or she did. Make your life-and-death choices beyond what the playwright has given you. Improvise, using your words. It is not important to remember all the dialogue. Continue your powerful reading. Finish the scene. As you break character and look at the auditor and say "thank you," notice how impressed he is by you. Hear him say something wonderful to you. Overhear him say to his A.D. to put your name on the callback list. Be proud of yourself for a job well done.

AUDITIONING FOR COMEDY

First of all, comedy *is* drama! Those characters up there are not having a great time laughing it up. They are in the midst of all sorts of conflicts precipitating trauma, tension, stress, anxiety, fear, pain, hurt, humiliation, anger, and beyond. The audience is having a great time laughing it up while a great deal of suffering can be going on up there on that stage or screen.

It is imperative that you know if you are auditioning for comedy or drama. Too many actors don't! Often, it is virtually impossible for the actor to ascertain from reading the sides if the script is comedy or drama. Either the sides don't reflect the comedic qualities well or the material is inferior and the so-called comedy is mediocre. Often, however, the comedy is genuine, but the actor doesn't recognize and comprehend the humor. As comedy writers and directors say, "You have to know where the funny is." They are referring to actors. If, in fact, a legitimately funny piece of material is before you and you don't recognize it as funny, you are going to have a difficult time getting professional work even in drama because *all* good drama has humor—that is, subtle tones of absurdity and irony. If you don't get the out-and-out bold comedy, what will happen to the inconspicuous and ethereal humor alive and in wait for the actor at the audition?

The novelist writes the entire book. The playwright writes half a play and is equal partners with the actor. The screenwriter controls less of his work because of the director, the camera, and the editor. Many Hollywood directors mangle and destroy the irony and absurdity in a play when turning it into a film.

Three examples of plays where the writer's contribution to the humor is "situational" and the actor's "behavioral" are *Burn This* by Lanford Wilson, *Extremities* by William Mastrosimone, and *Orphans* by Lyle Kessler. On paper, much of the humor of these plays and hundreds of others would be nonexistent to the average reader. The actor must not be the average reader! A serious piece of dramatic literature, replete with truth at its most heightened, is severe, drastic, and outrageous, and imbued with irony and absurdity that the actor *must* recognize during his or her preparation and performance.

These plays deal with deprivation, death, loneliness, alienation, terror, love, rejection, and violence. They have no comedic laugh lines, yet night after night, audiences have been doubled up with laughter—when they aren't crying or cringing with fear. The actor is to be fully credited!

The character breakdown should tell you if the script is comedy or drama. If you don't know which it is, ask the monitor. The writer has written what he believes to be a comedy or a drama containing comedic situations. He expects the actor to recognize "the funny."

You must bring your own personal sense of comedy to all readings. I don't care how funny the material is, if the actor lacks humor, the material will bomb and the audience won't laugh. If the material is devoid of humor but the actor is empowered with a keen sense of absurdity, irony, and "the funny," the audience will laugh. And it won't be a cheap laugh either. The actor is being honest with himself and the material. He is not being self-serving or self-indulgent. He is responding organically to the situation and servicing the play fully.

You don't have to make people fall down laughing to do comedy effectively, but you must be aware of and respond to the irony and absurdity in life and most certainly on the page, in order to service the writer's humor and his intention to evoke laughter from the audience. The laughs are often for the actor doing the listening, not the one doing the talking. Therefore, you must learn to be an "aggressive" listener and communicate that you hear every word, are assimilating it all, and are reacting to every bit of what you are hearing. The audience members often take their cue from the listener onstage. The audience is listening *with* you and your response feeds them. It's almost as if you are manipulating the audience. This is completely acceptable. The audience *wants* to be manipulated. Even your first audience: the auditors!

Keep the action going, apply a vigorous commitment to voice, and use the fourth wall fully to share your face with the audience, especially while listening so that you can guide them into hysterical laughter. The writer will adore you.

Creative Visualization Exercise: AUDITIONING FOR COMEDY

Prepare for the exercise. Visualize yourself auditioning for stage, screen, or television comedy. Your choice. Conjure up a funny script, one you are familiar with, or create your own! Do the reading, using all your comedic timing and abilities. Fight hard for what you need from the other character and project fully. Hear laughter from the auditors. (I always scream with laughter at an audition at anything funny.) Continue your scene, and when you are finished, have them applaud your performance. Everyone in that room is in a better mood now than when you first arrived to audition—all because of you. You brought a burst of humanity into their lives. You have given a great gift to them, and in turn you shall receive a callback.

AUDITIONING FOR COMMERCIALS

Auditions for commercials are generally held at the advertising agency. You will be given copy (the text of the commercial) to read. Give yourself about fifteen minutes to look over the copy and make your choices. There are no opposites in acting for the commercial. With very little exception, there is no irony and absurdity in the dialogue and no hidden inner life meanings. You are praising a product that you sincerely love. You will be addressing yourself to another character or to a camera. The monitor will give you directions.

You will read with a reader, or you might be instructed to read directly into the camera. See one person from your life in your mind's eye who you must communicate with regarding this remarkable product, and have a strong need for this person to believe you and want to go right out and buy it.

Never talk to a camera! Talk to a person. Turn the camera into a person.

Don't forget to ask in advance about the character's background so that you can dress accordingly.

Creative Visualization Exercise: AUDITIONING FOR COMMERCIALS

If you are interested in doing commercials, prepare to do this exercise. Pick a product. One that you are familiar with and think well of. Visualize yourself before a video camera in a television studio. The video lens is the person to whom you are talking and trying to persuade to buy this product. Use a person from your real life whom you genuinely would want to have this product. Sell it to him or her. It will enhance his or her life. Be sincere and self-assertive, but humble too. Be positive about yourself, the product, and the world around you. (Advertisers want their spokespersons to project happiness and good mental health). Convince your friend that life will be more rewarding with this product on the shelf. Have fun with this.

AUDITIONING FOR SOAP OPERA AND SITCOM (SITUATION COMEDY)

The soap and sitcom director is basically a technical director, not an actor's director. This means that the director will not work with you on your acting or your part. He or she will direct where you should stand, which camera to play to, and all physicality, so at the audition the auditors expect you to demonstrate that you will require no assistance with your acting.

Often, an assistant to the casting director places one actor after the other before a video camera, instructs each to do his or her monologue or cold reading, and immediately dismisses the actor. The casting director views the video at a later time and makes decisions regarding callbacks without ever seeing the actor in person. It is not necessary to see the actor offscreen. The audience never will either!

At times, the casting director will personally see you and audition you, but you will not work in front of a camera until your callback. Sometimes you will be granted an interview first, and perhaps an audition will be scheduled for the future.

For soap opera, it could be advantageous to pick up the sides a few days in advance and memorize your lines. The auditors might be impressed by this because in soap, new lines must be learned each day, and if you convey to them that you are quick to memorize, you'll get an extra point.

For camera work, you probably will not meet the director until the first day of shooting. You will be hired by the casting director.

Creative Visualization Exercise:
AUDITIONING FOR SOAP AND SITCOM

Prepare for the exercise. Pick a soap opera program or a sitcom. Audition for whichever one you want to be on and for the character you want to play. Visualize yourself in the television studio on the set reading the part. Improvise the dialogue, the situation, the events, and the relationship between the characters. Be there. Do a five-minute reading. Reenact scenes that you have viewed on television and have longed to do. Now is your time. You're on! Play the part. It's your fantasy—your dream. Play opposite the actors you have been watching in these shows. You are now one of them, the newest star among them.

THE DIFFERENCE BETWEEN AUDITIONING FOR FILM AND THEATER

As far as your preparation is concerned, there is no difference between auditioning for film and theater. For both theater and film auditions, the auditors must see strong commitment to character and relationship, emotional power, and communication.

When you are auditioning for theater, think of the other character as being across the room. You must speak up so that he or she can really hear you. The auditors will also know that you can be heard in the last row of the last balcony.

When you are auditioning for film, think of the other character as standing right alongside of you. There is no need to project a strong theater voice. However, the camera picks up what you are thinking, so during your preparation, work diligently on those inner life choices. I cringe each time I hear an actor say that he or she should "take it in" or "bring it down" or "close it up" for film auditions. It is precisely because of these words that so many actors fail at their film auditions. The level of passion and intensity should not be less for film auditions.

You should not be moving about and physicalizing for theater or film. Stay put and use that wonderful body of yours as a prop.

Watch your favorite film actors. Study them closely. Notice how they always have something going on within them: an attitude, a response, a smile, a point of view beyond their dialogue. Without these personal inner life choices and responses, they would not be interesting and genuine. The camera reveals a fraud instantly.

In film, you are playing to an audience just as you

would in a play. You don't look at the camera any more than you would make eye contact with a live audience unless you are directed to "break" the fourth wall.

As an example, during the famous scene at the Harmonia Gardens in the stage version of *Hello, Dolly!*, Carol Channing made eye contact at each performance with a female member of the audience seated down center. Dolly Levi and Horace Vandergelder are at their table and she is dishing food onto his plate as she talks to him, but her eyes are focused on the woman in the audience. This brilliant bit of staging created a communion between the two women that spread throughout the entire female half of the audience, inducing much laughter.

In a one-person play, the actor often makes eye contact with members of the audience. In a comedy film, occasionally as a silly bit, the actor will look right into the lens for a moment (à la John Belushi and Eddie Murphy) to connect with the audience. However, the most important thing about working before a camera is to forget it is there and go about the business of acting.

Your initial reading for a film may or may not be taped. Very often at the callback you will read with the star if there is to be a scene between the two of you, even if your part is a small one. Stars want to be sure that they like the actor's work and there is a compatibility. But stars additionally want to be assured that they will still shine in the scene. Film stars often have the power to hire or reject an actor.

In theater, the writer is king (or queen). Contractually, he or she usually has the final say in casting. However, with the exception of a few continually produced playwrights, most will go with the director's choices.

In film, the writer has nothing to do with casting. It is rare when one writer is given credit on a film. Some directors are major contributors in the writing of the script. In Hollywood, the writer is the low man on the totem pole, but he is paid an astronomical figure for his efforts, unlike his New York theatrical counterpart. The huge sums of money paid to the film writer do not guarantee an onscreen credit, however. Many screenwriters go to arbitration with The Writer's Guild to prove that at least 50 percent of the production script is their work, as compared to the script originally submitted. Some writers are paid huge sums of money for a script that the public will never see. The film will be shot, but a distributor can't be secured so the film is "canned"; it literally stays in a can on a shelf.

THE MONOLOGUE AUDITION

With the monologue audition, you have every luxury. You may take as long as you choose to rehearse, though the piece should be no longer than two minutes.

A monologue is a two-, or three-, or thousand-character scene. The other character or characters happen to not be saying anything for a minute or two. You are doing the talking; they are doing the listening.

Your monologue is not from the play you are auditioning for; therefore, you are not obliged to service the playwright's play fully as you must do in a cold reading. You must use the monologue as a vehicle to showcase you, the actor. It must work for you, not you for it.

The best way to look for monologues is *not* to look for monologues! For the love of Williams, Pinter, Wasserstein, and Durang, stop leafing through those pages in search of those speeches! You are cheating yourself by overlooking rich and energetic dialogue, relationships, and events that are in the here and now—events that are in the present—and involve the other character(s) in the scene.

Notice that speeches or long blocks of dialogue out of a play by and large consist of telling and recalling an action that took place already. The material deals with the past, not with the here and now. Moreover, this sort of piece doesn't allow you to connect with the other character(s) in the scene. You are not able to create a strong relationship because you are only telling a story. The material is essentially a memory piece.

When you are being seen by auditors, you want to show as much of your ability as possible. Simply telling a story—which is what you do in most traditional monologues—prevents this from happening and does not allow you to work with your full strengths as an actor. After such a speech, the auditors will turn to each other as your picture is placed on the "no" pile and say, "We don't know what this actor has to offer." I consider these words worse than saying we didn't like your work. For all I know, you might be a very intelligent and interesting actor, but with that material, how can I tell? The memory piece does not service you at all. It has no sense of immediacy, and the result is characterless and insipid.

By choosing material that consists of events (regarding the relationship between the characters) that are current, in the here and now, you have the opportunity to expose more of your abilities. You are creating a sense of urgency and emotional action. You can use your character's need to communicate right away to the other character(s) in the scene. Through your relationship and communication with the other character(s), the auditors are able to see your acting range.

We want to believe everything you are saying. Show us that you want to be up there and want to communicate with your audience. Reveal a generosity of spirit and do not be afraid of taking charge of the stage. It belongs to you for those two minutes. Your monologue is a vehicle to showcase *you*. You are presenting yourself in your own two-minute production.

When a television auditor requests a monologue, be careful about which monologue you choose. Some monologues can be offensive to television casting directors and agents. They are not accustomed to hearing "raw" material. Four-letter words or sexually explicit material is not done on commercial television, so you should not choose a monologue with those elements. It would be highly inappropriate, and your audience could be offended. On the other hand, theater casting directors and agents are only too aware of and used to raw material and are not easily shocked.

Do not write your own material unless you are a professional writer, because chances are you will not write a dramatic piece with the needed conflict.

The proper procedure for holding the audition is for you to be ushered into the assigned studio, theater, soundstage, office, storefront, living room, or back hall at the exact time your audition is scheduled. The auditors should already have your picture and resumé. If not, you will hand it to the director, agent, casting director, or stage manager on the way in. You will then stand before them, announce your name, the name of the play, and the name of the character. Do not "set up" the scene. In other words, do not explain what is happening in the scene or what has happened to lead up to this scene. Do not ask the auditors if they are familiar with the play. Perform for your audience. When it is over, give yourself a silent count of five to "allow the curtain to fall." Then break character, look at the auditors and say "thank you"—not a grateful thank you, but a courteous one.

Do not apologize when you are finished with your monologue. Too many actors do this. They shrug and giggle and look at us and say, "That's it." We get the strong feeling that they mean to say, "Sorry, but that's the best I can do and that's the only monologue I know how to do, and I know it's not really a good piece."

Now keep this thought in your mind: After the second time you have auditioned, you often are more experienced than the average auditor is in this procedure! Many auditors are inexperienced and are one-time auditors. Therefore, *you* know more than they do regarding the actor's process and how to best present yourself and perform for them!

I have covered everything regarding the monologue audition in my book, *The Perfect Monologue*. Much of what is in that book also relates to the cold reading and should be read in conjunction with this book.

THE ICE-COLD READING

When you arrive at the audition and the monitor hands you the sides and tells you to go right in and read immediately for the auditors with *no* preparation time, you are doing what is known as an ice-cold reading. Many of my former students report that they prefer ice-cold readings. We only work on them in the final two classes of each semester, but the preceding classes have prepared the actors for any and all obstacles. For many actors, the ice-cold reading is a living nightmare; for the more audacious, it represents a fascinating challenge. I have seen fine work done at auditions by actors who have done no preparation. In fact, some of the *best* readings I have seen have been ice cold!

The advantages of doing them include: you don't have time or the opportunity to intellectualize and to muck up your reading with weak choices (indeed, there are *no* choices); you are forced to intently listen to the other character's lines for the first time as actor *and* character, so you make discoveries for your character *during* the audition; there is a strong sense of immediacy, a stronger communication and commitment to the relationship; your responses are organic (honestly using your own personal reactions and sensibilities); you are more alert; and the auditors will give you the benefit of the doubt and be more tolerant of flaws.

The disadvantages of doing an ice-cold reading include: you can trip over or hesitate with words you can't pronounce or understand; there is no time to make any kind of choices; you can miss a cue; you have no sense of history for the character or the important events leading up to the confrontation; certain emotional responses that would have been appropriate for your character are not obvious until after you've spoken the dialogue; and you can muck up the whole reading out of fear.

Believe me when I tell you that the advantages far outweigh the disadvantages. Therefore, giving an intelligent and appealing reading under these circumstances is not an impossibility. In fact, it's easier than you think.

If you are one of the brave and wish to do an ice-cold reading, it is important for you to communicate to your auditors that you have not had time to look over the sides. Be prepared for the occasional auditor who will grant you the time. In your most humble manner, insist that it is perfectly all right with you and that since you're already up there, you'll give it a try.

Do *not* tell them that you prefer to do an ice-cold reading. Let them think that you, the professional actor, can handle any variance, that you are flexible and easy to work with and make no demands (until you get the part, that is).

They must know if your reading is ice cold so that if and when you trip over a line, miss a cue, or incorrectly pronounce a word, they will understand and absolve you of your sins.

You actually have a better chance of getting a callback if you do an ice-cold reading *and* the auditors are cognizant of this fact, because despite some minor infractions on your part during the reading, the auditors more often than not say to each other, "For an ice-cold reading, this was damn good! Can you imagine what he would have been able to do with this scene if he had prepared! Let's have him back and see what he can do with preparation." I've heard these words dozens of times.

To "prepare" for an ice-cold reading, arrive five minutes before your appointment to check in. See what the names of the characters are and say, as character, "Today is the most important day in my life. [The other character] is the most important person in my life. Today is the day I've *got* to change my life and [the other character] *must* help me."

Say these words immediately before your reading. You can say them as you are walking into the audition room. During your short exchange with the auditors to let them know this is an ice-cold reading, your thought process as character will be interrupted. Pick it up once more and give yourself a few seconds before you begin the reading.

Remind yourself again of the importance of the day and the other character. You will be making your discoveries along the way during the reading.

Don't do your homework in front of the auditors. The last thing auditors want to look at, even under these circumstances, is an actor preparing. But allow yourself a few seconds to conjure a sense of importance, immediacy, and relationship. Assume the other character is someone you care about more than anyone and that you desperately need something from him.

Let your left thumb guide your eye from line to line so that even under these circumstances you can take your eye off the page from time to time. Concentrate and listen to what the other character is saying. If you can, take a sneak peek forward on the page but not at the expense of interrupting your verbal rhythm. Remember to slow down so that you can make your discoveries. Never panic if you go up on a word (make a mistake). The auditors almost expect that this will happen during an ice-cold reading, and they are forgiving.

If you do not wish to do an ice-cold reading and the monitor tells you to read immediately for the auditors, first ask the monitor if you could have a few minutes to prepare. If the response is no, proceed into the audition room, and when you are before the auditors, tell them that you were instructed to read without any time to look over the sides. Then ask if it is possible to take a few minutes. The auditors will respond in one of two ways. One is to register surprise that you were given no time and grant it to you despite what the monitor told you; often they will admonish the monitor. The other is to concur with the monitor, knowing that because of limited time and so many appointments, they must proceed quickly. In your most congenial manner, convey that you certainly understand. Give yourself a few seconds to "prepare" and begin your reading.

Often the monitor speeds things up a bit because he or she is anxious to go home or does not want to work overtime. The monitor is thinking of him or herself. You must consider your needs also and assert yourself.

Remember what *all* plays are about: love, life, and death. You are fighting for your life. You desperately need something from the other character, the most important person in your life. You will find out what it is as you continue the reading.

Creative Visualization Exercise: AUDITIONING FOR THE ICE-COLD READING

Prepare for the exercise. Visualize yourself showing up five minutes before your scheduled appointment to check in and pick up your sides. You have already made the decision to do an ice-cold reading today. You know the name of your character and the name of the other character. You have a bit of information about them from the character breakdown. You are ready to go in there and burn up that stage with your reading. The monitor tells you to go in. You repeat to yourself that today is the most important day in your life and [the other character] is the most important person in your life. Today is the day that you *must* change your life and [the other character] *must* help you. You are before the auditors and you make your announcement to them that you didn't get to look at the sides because the monitor sent you right in, but this is okay with you and you are ready. The director tells you to take a few minutes if you'd like and work on the sides. You respond by saying that since you're up there and you don't want to slow down their schedule, you'll just do it now and do the best you can. You begin your reading with the reader. You feel the sense of importance that you've brought to the reading. You are making the reading very conversational. Your left thumb guides your eyes down the page to each line so you feel comfortable taking your eyes off the page. You begin to discover what is taking place on the page. There are no gaps in emotional action because of the importance and immediacy you brought to the scene. It's as if you worked on the pages for a half hour. You are making all the discoveries and are completely involved in the relationship. You are aggressively listening to the other character and responding organically. When you come to the end, you feel exhilarated. You offer your thanks to the reader and auditor. You leave knowing that you were successful doing an ice-cold reading. It was an adventurous experience for you. You look forward to doing it again, very soon.

LOOKING OUT FOR
YOUR INTERESTS

In this business you must often protect yourself from those whom you most rely on, need, and trust: your agent and your director. They share the responsibility to accommodate you and minister to you: the agent to help advance your career and reap the monetary benefits of your successes, and the director to nurture and guide you into a smashing performance in his or her production. They also have the power to sabotage and invalidate you—if you allow them to! I will present examples and provide you with protective measures.

HOW NOT TO BE FIRED
AFTER YOU HAVE BEEN
HIRED

You and your loved ones celebrate. Rehearsals commence in two weeks, and you begin to arrange your life around the production, your first major one!

Then you get a phone call from your agent telling you that the producer changed his mind. The deal is off. You are unhired. Need I explain how you would feel?

The reason you are no longer a part of the production is that your agent negotiated you right out of the contract!

After the decision is made to hire you for the part, the producer contacts your agent to discuss salary and the terms of the contract. He tells your agent that he will pay you AEA or SAG minimum, which at this writing is respectively $925 and $1,620 per week. I don't consider this to be a paltry sum of money, especially since this is to be your first featured part in an important play or film. I have yet to be informed by one actor that this amount of money would be unacceptable under these conditions. The agent, however who is going to receive 15 percent of your earnings (let's assume AEA wages for this example), will be earning his $138.75 a week from your paycheck, but he decides that $200 or so would be a much more desirable figure for his weekly take. He tells the producer that you, his client, will not work for minimum and must have $1,400 per week. The producer argues that minimum is all he can pay and stay within his budget. He addresses the fact that it is your first time in a major production and in fact your part is not the lead. He says he can hire another actor who was also perfect for the part. The agent is unrelenting, causing the producer to finally tell him that he will go with the other actor. The agent calls you and tells you that the producer changed his mind and that is *all* he tells you! Two hundred dollars is better than $0, but greed and ego have tarnished his common sense. Obviously the agent doesn't have *you* in mind.

My advice is to communicate loud and clear to your agent as soon as you are told that you have a callback that you are very willing and able to accept minimum wage.

HOW NOT TO BE FIRED
DURING THE REHEARSAL

Most actors show up at the first rehearsal with script in hand and a mind barren and devoid of choices and ideas for the character, relationships, and events in the script. Although this is the first cast rehearsal, it should not be the first *rehearsal*! Start rehearsing immediately after being hired. Get off book as soon as possible. You do not require the presence of your fellow actors or director. Make your inner life choices for all your scenes and make choices for the characters in your scenes. The worst way to show up at the first cast rehearsal is with a mind as blank as an empty blackboard. Be filled with choices and prejudices. Be prepared to replace them with different choices as you make discoveries throughout your rehearsals. Do not *ever* put yourself in the position of having a blank mind.

During the rehearsals, you will replace choices as you progress and make further discoveries about your character and the relationships. Be very willing and open to make these changes. This is one way to ensure your tenure in the production.

Many directors think of actors as being disposable. If you don't get a hook into the character within the first week of rehearsals, they will fire you and even have someone waiting in the wings before you are notified. They won't take the extra time to work with you and help you with acting problems. In more civilized areas of the world, directors feel a sense of obligation and responsibility to their actors.

Unfortunately, many directors are not capable of helping an actor! They simply don't know what to do with an actor who needs a little help. The director's background and training is concentrated on reading and analyzing plays, interpreting character, and creating the look of the production—costumes, lighting, props, and blocking— with technicians and designers. Conspicuously missing is an ability to help actors to resolve acting problems. The actors are on their own.

The director certainly cannot get into the head of actors and make inner life choices for them, and no director should have to spoon-feed actors. The director is the frame. The actor, the picture. The director cannot and should not attempt to get in there with you. He must guide, nurture, and direct you to make your own inner life choices. The director must never make them for you. You are the artist and the art. You must paint your own brush-strokes, but you often need a guiding hand. Too often, there is an absence of guidance, nurturing, and direction.

If you find yourself in this situation, rush to a drama coach whose work you respect and pay for an hour or more of private instruction. Do not reveal to your director that you have sought help from another. The director who is ill-equipped and or unwilling to work with you will resent "outside interference" with one of "his" actors. Also, let the director assume that your good work came from you with no help.

A director should allow and encourage you to experiment with various interpretations at your will, at least during the first couple of weeks of rehearsals. If you are cursed with one who forbids you to deviate from his interpretation (which he presents as dogma), or perhaps one who gives you the freedom to examine alternatives and then pronounces your efforts and results to be inappropriate, all is not lost.

If you *truly* believe that your interpretation is the right one but the director clearly will not tolerate any changes, do not pursue your case. Appear as if you are submitting to the director's wishes.

You must not aspire to "win" against the director simply for the sake of winning. Everyone will lose! Your purpose is to present the most glorious and honest performance you can by opening night, one appropriate to the character and events in the play. Good directors know what they are talking about, so do listen and hear them out. But if you, in total honesty, in your heart of hearts, believe that your interpretation is the correct one, I suggest the following procedure.

At your rehearsal following the director's pronouncement, do it that way. At each rehearsal thereafter, incorporate something from your interpretation. Take it one step at a time. If the director says nothing, continue along this path. If he or she suddenly confronts you, take one step back. Continue this way until your opening night or the shoot. If the director says nothing more about your performances at the rehearsals, you have the pleasure of knowing that you were indeed correct in your judgment. By ceasing to interfere, the director indicates approval.

It is an impossible task for you to be brilliant in a part if you cannot create with your own personal sensibilities. There is no such thing as compromise for an artist. It must be done your way. You must intelligently evaluate the inner workings of the character. The writer has provided the peripheral components. Whatever your inner life choices are, they must be attuned to the writer's character. The writer also will not compromise.

Directors love to talk plays to death instead of getting you up on your feet and solving problems through your acting, experimentation, and the resulting discoveries. Analyzing and intellectualizing is a waste of time for everyone. Unfortunately, this is what most directors do best.

When you have a problem in a scene where you can't justify an action (you can't connect with what is happening), a good director should encourage you to improvise the scene in your own words with your fellow actor; naturally, this will result in some new plot directions. If your director does not suggest doing this, take it upon yourself to ask permission to do an improv.

Another way to overcome a problem in a scene is for you to read your line as written and then say the same thing in your own words. Your partner should do the same. You might want to do the entire scene in this manner. In fact, you could do the entire script this way. It is time-consuming but well worth it. By working this way, you will be able to break through, as character to character and actor to actor. More discoveries will take place, new insights will be revealed, and barriers will be broken down.

Your director should have a complete run-through of the play by the end of the second week of rehearsals, no matter what condition the play is in. And often it will be in awful condition, but no matter. The actors need a sense of continuity as soon as possible. Many directors wait until it is too late in the rehearsal to call a run-through. The actors and the entire production suffer. Take it upon yourself at the end of ten days of rehearsals to suggest or even request that your director call a run-through.

During rehearsals, you can be fired from a production for reasons other than acting problems. Do not badmouth the script, director, playwright, producer, the producer's wife, his girlfriend, the stage manager, your fellow actors, or anyone on the production staff. No one wants to hear negativity and someone will tell on you. Do not trust your stage manager. He or she is representing the director, playwright, and producer, not you! Be professional in *every* way; the stage manager will respect you.

SUBMIT YOURSELF

Read the character breakdowns in the trade papers. If you relate to a part but cannot get an agent to submit you, go to the audition and try to get a word with an auditor. Don't hesitate to go right up to him, especially if the opportunity presents itself. For instance, stop him while he's on a break and state that you want the opportunity to audition because you *know* the part is perfect for you and you are perfect for the part. Beg him to grant you just two minutes. Say to him, "If I'm lousy, you can throw me right out! And if I'm great, everybody comes out ahead. What have you got to lose? Just two minutes! That's all I'm asking!"

You would be amazed how many actors have gotten auditions this way. I have granted auditions with this approach if the actor looked to me to be in the right ballpark and had a decent resumé. Three of today's major stars said those words to me several years ago.

Sometimes it works if you simply show up at the audition and hang around. This is especially effective if several productions are casting in one place and the waiting room is in the center, surrounded by the audition rooms. Actors have been known to get an audition by just making themselves noticed in the waiting room—not by doing anything crazy, just by being there. A monitor will mention to the auditor that there is a very interesting looking actor who fits the type they are seeking. Or the auditor will walk through and spot an interesting face and request a look at the resumé.

A major star once had himself gift wrapped and delivered to an agent who had been refusing to see him.

A Hollywood superstar once followed me and my playwright companion around a party for an entire evening, begging us to grant him an audition. We finally gave in just to get rid of him.

Some actors show up at agencies in person, despite warnings not to walk through the door without an appointment. Once in a while, however, casting directors or agents will walk by, take a look, and like what they see. The actor is invited into the office and is interviewed and auditioned.

I counseled an actor once to write a letter to the star of a Broadway play, who also happened to be the playwright. This multilevel star was leaving the show and a replacement was being sought. My actor couldn't get an appointment with the casting director, so he took my advice and wrote a short letter requesting an audition. Not only had he seen the play more than once, but he loved and identified with the character. He asked for his two minutes. A few days later he received a response and an appointment to audition. He made it to the final callback. He lost the part to an actor who had a stronger track record, one who had already been on Broadway. This same actor couldn't get an agent to submit him for any commercials, so he submitted himself to all the casting directors in all the advertising agencies, and he wound up doing three major national commercials. Some agent lost a lot of money.

An actor once said to me that he didn't want to be too aggressive or obnoxious. I replied, "Then what are you doing in this business? How do you expect to get any-where?"

Creative Visualization Exercise: HOW NOT TO BE FIRED

Prepare for the exercise. Visualize yourself at an audition, performing brilliantly. Choose the play or film you are auditioning for and the character. A few days after the audition, your agent informs you that you got a callback. Clearly convey to him or her that you will gladly accept minimum wage, especially because this will be your first major production. Furthermore, your part, while interest-ing, is not the lead. See yourself at the callback, once more turning in a brilliant performance. You are hired! You sign the contract and go into rehearsals. You like the director, but when you begin to get deeper into the part, you realize he is not going to put in the time to work with you, so you run to your drama coach. You get the help you need and your director praises your work. At one point during the rehearsals, you suggest that you and the other actor in the scene do an improv, and your director agrees that it is a wonderful idea. You do it, and indeed, the scene becomes clearer to you and you feel completely comfortable in areas where before you felt ill at ease. You are lucky because your director calls a run-through before two weeks of rehearsals, and you are grateful to him for being insightful. You get to your dress tech (last rehearsal) and then your opening night. You and the play triumph.

Creative Visualization Exercise:
SUBMIT YOURSELF

Prepare for the exercise. Visualize being courageous and brave enough to go out there and make sure that you do everything in your power to get those auditions, short of doing something immoral or illegal! You show up at audition spaces and let yourself be seen. You approach casting directors and tell them how right you are for the part. You ask them for just two minutes of their time, and more often than not, it is granted. Visualize being creative in getting to agents and casting directors.

THE POWER OF
THE ACTOR

You possess power that no one in this business seems to want you to be aware of. Knowledge of this power can help you in your auditions immeasurably, so I will explain what I mean.

The following occurs at least once in every production: We are auditioning actors and have seen six of them back to back over the last thirty or forty minutes. All six performances are dreadful! We are desolate, depressed, drained, bored, and worried. The producer hisses, "I'll never be able to raise the money for this show." The director mutters, "Maybe I should have gone with the other play offered to me." The playwright wails, "Did I write this garbage?" They turn to the casting director and ask, "What the hell are you doing to us?"

Then, the seventh actor is before us. He does his reading. He is wonderful! Alive, intelligent, communicative, humorous, appealing, committed to character with emotional action and a strong sense of humanity. We love him! We thank him and he leaves. The producer announces, "I won't have any trouble raising cash for this production!"

The director gushes, "I knew I chose the right play!" The playwright beams, "I knew I was a genius!" Then they all turn to the casting director and chant, "You are a brilliant casting director!"

One good performance cancels out six bad ones. That to me is power! What did this actor do that the other six did not? They all were auditioning for the same part and reading from the same scene. Only one made life-and-death choices with honesty and *shared* them with us. He truly wanted to be open and communicate and expose his vulnerability, and he didn't allow anything to get in his way during his preparation or the performance. He took risks and was not afraid to fail. *If you are afraid of failure, you will fail.*

We desperately need intelligent actors—and we love them. They make our work exciting. It is nothing less than thrilling after one or two lines of dialogue are spoken and a rush of excitement permeates the very air around us because we know we have found "the one."

Another example of the actor's power has to do with how you, during your reading at the audition, can influence the playwright to create a better character.

You finish your reading, are thanked, and you leave. The playwright then says, "That actor was absolutely right. Now I understand the character." The playwright goes home to rewrite and create a better character! What did you do? You didn't change a word! Well, what you did was make more interesting and stronger inner life choices than the playwright did, and you gave the work more meaning. You took bigger risks than he did.

You were successful because you had two vital ingredients—the facility to make life-and-death choices and the willingness to communicate.

You can't ever be "the one" if you walk through life with blinders on. It is perfectly acceptable to the world if one chooses alienation in life, but for acting, one must be deeply involved. By this I simply mean being aware. You don't have to be "on" every moment or be the life of the party or have hordes of friends and lovers. Indeed, many major theater and film stars, considered to be some of

America's finest actors, are actually dull company, *but* they are listening and observing behavior and share a passionate curiosity about life. They don't necessarily communicate strongly and reveal themselves until they have a script in their hands—and then—watch the magic begin!

Let the magic begin with you!

PART 2

Creative Visualization
for the Character

CHAPTER SEVEN

EXAMPLES OF PLAYS USING CREATIVE VISUALIZATION IN PREPARATION FOR THE CALLBACK

All the actors who auditioned for the following plays in my workshop classes had total commitment to their characters and to the relationships. They made honest and strong choices. They were aggressive listeners and responded with emotional vigor, exposing their vulnerabilities and humanity; therefore, there was integrity and humor in all the performances and scenes. They knew what they were fighting for and used their fantasies and dreams to expose a strong and appealing stage presence. Each performance was worthy of a callback.

As you'll see in the following examples, I worked with each actor on creative visualization and making the strongest possible choices for their characters. Using what background we gathered from the sides, I coached these actors to help them successfully incorporate real-life events, fantasies, and goals—things that they, as individuals, could relate to—into the choices they made for their characters. Obviously, they had the advantage of working with another person, a coach, while you will work independently. The goal of presenting these examples is to get you to see how you—working on your own—can arrive at these kinds of positive, sky's-the-limit choices in visualizing for your character. Once you've mastered the art of making the strongest choices, you'll get the callback.

Danny and the Deep Blue Sea
by John Patrick Shanley

The actors are Kathy and Grant. The characters are ROBERTA and DANNY. She is fighting for love from him even though she is in a rage and appears to be wanting him to leave. The actress (Kathy) understands that this rage is a defense mechanism and that although ROBERTA is guilt-ridden and feels she should be punished because of her past incestuous relationship with her father, she also craves love. She is fighting for DANNY, who she knows is prone to violence, to protect and love her forever. If ROBERTA were forced to evaluate her true feelings, she would know this. The actress *must* know this.

ROBERTA

Ginger: Roberta, I want you to see your future as you wish it to be and in fact as it *will* be, and I want you to tell me step-by-step each wonderful and happy event starting right now in this room with Danny. If you could have anything in the world right now after this conversation with him, what would it be?

Kathy, I want you to make choices for yourself, as Roberta, that come from *your* wishes, fantasies, and desires. What happens next? Talk to me in character.

Roberta: Well, we get married.

Ginger: Right now in this room? You're rushing ahead a little. First tell me what happens in the here and now.

Roberta: I want him to convince me that I am a good person who deserves a better life and I need to know that he won't continue to be a violent person.

Ginger: This is creative visualization. You don't have to say you "want him to." He *does* convince you.

Roberta: He tells me I am a good person who was my father's victim and I am not to be blamed for what I did with him. He also convinces me that I'm the first woman he's ever loved and he will never hurt me and will change his ways and not get into fights anymore.

Ginger: And then what?

Roberta: He asks me to marry him, but I'm afraid.

Ginger: In creative visualization, there are no negatives and opposites. You were fearful all along, but now he convinces you and you begin to lose your fears. For the first time in your life you feel deserving, protected, and loved. What other emotion are you feeling that is a new one for you?

Roberta: Happy.

Ginger: Yes. And then what happens?

Roberta: We plan our wedding.

Ginger: Kathy, now I'm talking to you. If you were to get married, what kind of wedding would you like to have?

Kathy: Me, personally? The actress?

Ginger: Yes, you the actress, not Roberta.

Kathy: Well, my aunt lives in an eighteenth-century house way out on Long Island, with rock gardens, a rose garden, a grape arbor, and a gazebo right near a stream. I've always thought how great it would be to have a wedding there.

Ginger: Roberta, you are getting married in your
            aunt's gardens at the gazebo near the stream. Kathy,
            what kind of dress would you love to wear for your
            wedding if you were getting married?

Kathy: I actually would like to make my own wed-
            ding dress. I sew very well and make most of my
            clothing, and I'd love to design my own wedding
            gown. I would love it to be an off-the-shoulder chif-
            fon gown tucked at the waistline and belted with
            white satin ribbons, and the skirt would be long and
            billowy. I would wear a very large picture hat made
            from the chiffon with satin ribbons cascading down
            the back.

Ginger: Roberta, you are going to wear that dress at
            your wedding. Kathy, where would you love to go
            on your honeymoon?

Kathy: Paris. But we can't afford a trip to Europe!

Ginger: Remember that in creative visualization you
            can have anything you want. We have to find a way
            for you to afford it. For instance, this aunt of yours
            might give you the money for the trip or perhaps it
            would be her wedding present to you besides the
            use of her home and grounds for the wedding. She
            loves you, so it is her pleasure and she can afford it.
            You go off to Paris for a glorious week. Now
            Roberta, where are you two going to live?

Roberta: Well, he moves into my place, which is a
            private apartment in my parents' house, and there is
            no rent.

Ginger: Tell me how it is for both of you living there
            and how your parents feel about Danny.

Roberta: I couldn't believe it, but they actually liked
            him when they met him, and he thought they were
            sort of cool, even though he knew what my father
            had done. It's like Danny forgave him, so I was able
            to also. Living there was okay, and Danny and I
            were able to save money.

Ginger: Are you working?

Roberta: Yes, as a seamstress.

Ginger: Roberta, how would you like to take a few

classes in design at the Fashion Institute of Technology design school?

Roberta: Who, me? Yeah, I sure would.

Ginger: Danny insists that you do when he sees how beautifully you design and sew. You take the classes, and in no time your designs are getting attention. What does Danny do for a living?

Roberta: He drives a truck.

Ginger: After you finish the courses, you get a job in a top Seventh Avenue design house. How does this sound to you?

Roberta: It sounds wonderful.

Ginger: Kathy, does this scenario appeal to you?

Kathy: It certainly does.

Ginger: Roberta, how do you feel about Danny being away at times because of his truck driving.

Roberta: I hate it. I want him to be home with me every night, not driving to other states.

Ginger: What would you like him to be doing?

Roberta: I'd like him to work right here in New York. What I'd really love is if we could work together.

Ginger: Doing what?

Roberta: I could teach him about the fashion industry, and he could get involved in our own design business. If it wasn't for him, I wouldn't even be doing this right now.

Ginger: You're absolutely right. So what happens next?

Roberta: He quits his job. I take the money we've saved and get a bank loan and we open our own business and Danny runs it and does a damn good job and my designs sell like hotcakes and are featured in *Vogue* and all the fashion magazines and very wealthy women wear my clothing.

Ginger: Kathy, if you could live anywhere in New York, where would that be?

Kathy: I'd love to live in a brownstone in the West Village.

Ginger: Roberta, you and Danny buy a brownstone in

the West Village. Kathy, do you have any desire to travel?

Kathy: Of course. I'd love to visit places like Paris, Milan, Rome, London, and the Orient.

Ginger: Roberta, you and Danny take frequent trips abroad for business and pleasure. You go to Paris, Milan, Rome, London, and the Orient. Does this agenda excite you, Kathy?

Kathy: Are you serious? It sounds great!

Ginger: Roberta, you both get to relax with no work at times. Kathy, is there a warm-weather type of vacation that you wish you could go on?

Kathy: I've always wanted to go to the Greek islands.

Ginger: Roberta, you and Danny relax on a trip to the Greek islands. Kathy, if you had enough money to have a summer or vacation home, where would it be?

Kathy: Vermont. It's great in summer and winter.

Ginger: Roberta, you and Danny buy a beautiful vacation home in Vermont that you frequent often all year round. Kathy, what are your personal concerns regarding the world's problems?

Kathy: I wish I could have time and money to help save the rain forests and the environment.

Ginger: Roberta, you get very involved with saving the rain forests and the environment, and you are able to raise millions of dollars from your efforts. Kathy, when you are married, will you be wanting children?

Kathy: Absolutely. In fact, I want a large family.

Ginger: Roberta, you and Danny have five children. You continue to flourish in your business. You and Danny stay in love and have a beautiful relationship filled with romance, kindness, passion, and excitement.

Let's sum up this future. Danny convinces you that you deserve a happy life and that he will not be violent anymore. You and he marry in the beautiful gardens belonging to your aunt and you spend your honeymoon in Paris. Danny gets along fine with your folks and forgives your father, which you are able to do also. You live in your apartment in their home for a while rent-free, and both of you are able to save money each week. You are a seamstress, and Danny convinces you to go to the Fashion Institute, which you do, and soon you get a great job in a first-rate design house on Seventh Avenue and you are successful there. Danny quits his job driving a truck, and you both open your own design business, which he runs, and it is a huge success. Your dresses are in *Vogue* and are worn by wealthy women. You move to your own brownstone in the West Village, and you travel for business and pleasure throughout Europe and the Orient. You vacation in the Greek islands. You buy a vacation home in Vermont. You have five children. You work on behalf of saving the rain forests and the environment, and you raise millions of dollars. You and Danny have a continuing love affair throughout your lives. *This* is what you are fighting for!

DANNY

Although he has just met ROBERTA the night before, DANNY knows that he loves her and wants her to marry him. He's been knocking around getting into fights and feeling alienated from the world, and now sees a way to change his life. He doesn't care what ROBERTA has done before he met her. He is fighting for her love and her commitment to him.

Ginger: Danny, I want you to see your future as you wish it to be and in fact as it *will* be, and I want you to tell me step-by-step each wonderful and happy event starting right now in this room with Roberta. If you could have anything in the world right now after this conversation with her, what would it be?

Grant, I want you to make choices for yourself as Danny that come from *your* wishes, fantasies, and desires. What happens next? Talk to me in character.

Danny: I convince her to marry me.

Ginger: How does this affect your life, Danny?

Danny: I feel like I belong—like for the first time in my life, someone loves me and wants me. I feel that with Roberta's love, I can accomplish anything.

Ginger: What do you want to accomplish and how do you want to change your life?

Danny: I want to stop fighting with everybody, make peace with my mother, and get a better job than driving a truck.

Ginger: That's exactly what you do. And Roberta helps you in all these areas. What kind of job would you like? Grant, now I'm talking to you. If you were not an actor, can you consider what other means of work could satisfy you? Or would that be impossible because acting is the *only* work for you?

Grant: I really can't see myself doing anything else. It sort of has to be acting.

Ginger: Okay. Danny, you drive a truck and that's the only job you've ever had. I have a feeling that you haven't gone to the theater, but how about movies? Do you go to movies?

Danny: Yeah. I've seen plenty of movies.

Ginger: Have you ever thought about acting in any of them?

Danny: How did you know? I could really get into that. I even thought about taking acting lessons, but I thought, nah, I'd probably be laughed right out of class.

Ginger: Guess what, Danny. You tell this to Roberta, and she insists that you enroll in classes immediately. You do and you are not laughed right out of class. In fact, the teacher tells you that you are very talented and have a great look and if you stick with it, you can make it. How does that make you feel, Danny?

Danny: That's great. I feel great.

Ginger: You keep studying, have pictures taken, audition for agents, and one wants to handle you. You are submitted for commercials and soap opera and get work in both. Is this something you can relate to, Grant?

Grant: I'm drooling just thinking about it.

Ginger: In that case, you get the work, start making the bucks, and you are on your way. No more truck driving. Grant, what are your career goals? Where do you want to be down the road?

Grant: I want to do Broadway, but eventually I really want to do films in California.

Ginger: Danny, you get a part off Broadway, get rave reviews, and then get cast on Broadway where the reviews are even better. You are nominated for a Tony Award, and Hollywood comes calling offering you leads in films. You and Roberta move to the West Coast. Does this scenario appeal to you, Grant?

Grant: It couldn't be better. It's what I would kill for.

Ginger: Are you familiar with Los Angeles, Grant?

Grant: I was out there a couple of times. I sort of know my way around.

Ginger: If you could live anywhere in the Los Angeles area, where would you love to live, Grant?

Grant: On the beach at Malibu.

Ginger: Danny, you and Roberta buy a house on the beach at Malibu. You make your film and get the rave reviews there. You and Roberta are ecstatic, madly in love, and happier than you ever imagined you could be and this is what you are fighting for this day in Roberta's room.

Let's summarize the future. You convince Roberta to marry you. For the first time in your life, you belong—someone loves you. You now feel you can accomplish anything. You stop fighting and make peace with your mother. You study acting and start doing commercials and soaps. You give up truck driving. You then do off Broadway, Broadway, and then films. You and Roberta move to Los Angeles and buy a home on the beach at Malibu. You and she live in bliss and you continue to make films. *This* is what you are fighting for.

Elliot Loves by Jules Feiffer

The actors are Kim and Brian. The characters are JOANNA and ELLIOT. They are in a relationship, and JOANNA is now going to meet ELLIOT's friends for the first time and she is panic-stricken in case they don't like her. She is very insecure and is stalling for time before she allows herself to step into the elevator that will take them up to the friends' apartment. She desperately needs ELLIOT's help to save her from this traumatic meeting. She is fighting for his love to protect her and keep her safe.

JOANNA

Ginger: Joanna, I want to see your future as you wish it to be and in fact as it *will* be, and I want you to tell me step-by-step each wonderful and happy event starting right now in this lobby in Elliot's friends' building. If you could have anything in the world right now after this conversation with him, what would it be? Kim, I want you to make choices for yourself as Joanna that come from *your* wishes, fantasies, and desires. What happens next? Talk to me in character.

Joanna: He tells me we don't have to go upstairs. He says he loves me so much that he will not ever put me in a situation that I am afraid of.

Ginger: Okay. And then what?

Kim: I have to say that I really relate to what she is

going through. I had practically the same experience, and my boyfriend couldn't deal with it and told me to see a shrink.

Ginger: All right. Let's use that. Did you love your boyfriend?

Kim: Yes.

Ginger: Did you lose him?

Kim: Yeah. He broke up with me.

Ginger: Then you certainly know how it feels to be dumped. You know how it hurts. Do you wish you could have had the courage to go through with it and meet his friends?

Kim: I sure do. I'm still a little scared about too many things in life.

Ginger: Joanna, Elliot is very understanding and has patience with you. He encourages you to talk openly with him about your fears, and because you trust him you tell him to set up another evening with his friends, and this time you and he get in that elevator and go up to their apartment and you have a wonderful time. Now you tell me, Joanna, do they like you?

Joanna: They sure do. They make that very clear. And I like them and become close friends with two of his friends' wives.

Ginger: And then what happens?

Joanna: We have wonderful times together. We even go on vacations with his friends, and my relationship with Elliot grows and I lose all my fears and insecurities. Elliot and I talk about marriage.

Ginger: Kim, are you interested in marriage at this time in your life?

Kim: No, not right now. I don't think I'm ready for that yet.

Ginger: Then you and Elliot discuss it, but it's established by you that marriage is for down the road, not for now. Is he upset by this?

Joanna: Well, slightly. I am very flattered by his attitude, but he doesn't pressure me about it.

Ginger: Is your career very important to you?

Joanna: Very much so. Yes.

Ginger: What kind of work do you do?

Joanna: I am an actress.

Ginger: Have you worked professionally yet?

Joanna: I've done summer stock, two commercials, and a lot of off-off Broadway. I'm still studying.

Ginger: When you and Elliot socialize with his friends, how do you spend your evenings?

Joanna: We usually have dinner and go to the theater, which is naturally what I prefer doing more than anything else. I see more Broadway shows since I met Elliot because he can afford the price of the tickets.

Ginger: Does he like to go to the theater or is he doing it mostly for you?

Joanna: Well, he admitted that before me he didn't go so often, but he knows how much I want to go so he takes me. But he told me he enjoys it very much.

Ginger: You say you go on vacations. Kim, where would you most like to take a vacation?

Kim: I'd love to travel on the Orient Express.

Ginger: Joanna, you and Elliot go to Europe and take the Orient Express. When you come back from the trip, there is a call from your agent regarding an important audition. It's for off Broadway. You audition and get the part. Kim, does the thought of this excite you?

Kim: Absolutely.

Ginger: Joanna, Elliot and all his friends are in the audience opening night. You get a standing ovation and bravos. You've got it all. A great career, a nurturing lover, and marvelous friends. This is what you are fighting for in that lobby.

Let's summarize the future. Elliot protects you by taking the pressure off regarding your fears about meeting his friends. He has patience with you and encourages you to talk about your fears, which you do, and you are finally able to gather up the courage and meet them. They love you and you love them. You all socialize, doing dinners and going to the theater. You go on vacations together. You and Elliot take a trip on the Orient Express. You audition for an off-Broadway play and get the part. You get a standing ovation and bravos from Elliot, his friends, and the entire audience. You continue to perform off Broadway and on Broadway, and Elliot is always there for you. *This* is what you are fighting for.

ELLIOT

ELLIOT loves JOANNA very much, but she has little ways about her that drive him up a wall. He would love it if she could just relax and enjoy their relationship. He is fighting for her to love him enough to trust him and believe in him more and not create any problems in their relationship. I instruct Brian to begin the creative visualization.

Elliot: Joanna finally agrees to get into the elevator and come up to meet my best friends. We have a terrific time, and we get together with them lots of times. They like her just as I knew they would, and she likes them.

Ginger: What's the next event?

Elliot: Well, I want her to move in with me, but she's got two kids.

Ginger: What's the problem?

Brian: I have to say that I don't think I could be involved with a woman with kids at this time in my life. Maybe Elliot wouldn't mind, but it would bother me. So how do I handle this when you say we're supposed to personalize and go with the way we, the actors, feel?

Ginger: That's right. Your characters don't have to do, say, or think as you, the actor does, but when we get to creative visualization, that changes. So, Brian, what would you do if you fell in love with a woman with a couple of kids?

Brian: Well, I'd spend as much time as I could with her, and I guess I would even spend some time with her kids, and probably I could have fun with them and like them, but living with them! That's another story. So I would keep my apartment and explain to her the way I feel and hope that she would keep seeing me, and who knows, maybe one day it would all change and I would want to live with them all. Probably when I make it as an actor and could afford a really big place. Yeah, that would be all right. I might even want to marry her at that time. I think I could be married—someday. The important thing right now is, I don't want to lose her.

Ginger: Okay. Elliot, you and Joanna keep seeing each other. The relationship flourishes. You get along great with her kids. Elliot, what do you do for a living?

Brian: It didn't say what he did in the sides so I chose to be a lawyer.

Ginger: We have to deal with what your job is because you are the one who brought up that you are an actor who hasn't made it yet. Why did you decide to be a lawyer?

Brian: I have no idea. I have no interest in being a lawyer.

Ginger: Never choose to be what you have no interest in being. Most of you will choose to have your characters be actors, which is fine. You must create choices in creative visualization that excite you, the actor, and it is obvious that when it comes to your character's line of work, acting is the one that is the strongest choice. Remember, we are talking about creative visualization now, and we are talking about preparing for the callback. Once you get the part, you will be whatever the playwright has indicated the character is. In this situation, feel free to be whatever you want. And it seems quite clear what your profession should be.

Elliot: I am an actor!

Ginger: Of course you are. So what happens next?

Elliot: Well, I continue to study and audition and I get hired for a part.

Ginger: Brian, what are your career goals? What would be the most rewarding for you at this time? Getting a part on off Broadway, Broadway, television, or a film?

Brian: Broadway.

Ginger: Then why don't you tell me the details of this next glorious event? Tell me as Elliot.

Elliot: My agent submits me for a new David Mamet play opening on Broadway. I get the audition and read for a great part, I get the callback, and I get the part.

Ginger: Exciting to visualize this, isn't it? Especially if Mamet is a favorite of yours.

Brian: He is my favorite playwright.

Ginger: What happens next?

Elliot: Joanna and our friends come to the opening and the party. The notices come in and the critics love me! Everyone makes a big fuss over me, and I am so happy that I propose to Joanna.

Ginger: Does she accept?

Elliot: Yes. But we plan to wait awhile before getting married. I start doing commercials during the run of the play and other offers come in, but the one I accept is to do the film of the Mamet play. It gets shot right here in New York, which is great because I don't have to go to California. I prefer living and working in New York. So the money starts coming in and I can afford larger and better living quarters.

Ginger: Brian, where would you love to live in New York?

Brian: In Soho, in a huge loft.

Ginger: Elliot, you and Joanna buy a huge loft in Soho, get married, and you get one part after the other on Broadway and films, and you are asked by Mr. Mamet to be in all his plays and films as he writes them. *This* is what you are fighting for on this day in that lobby in front of the elevator that Joanna is frightened to step into.

Let's summarize the future. Joanna overcomes her insecurity, meets and loves your friends, as they do her. You and she have wonderful times together, and you enjoy her children. She puts no pressure on you to escalate the relationship. You continue to live separately. You are an actor and you audition for the new David Mamet play on Broadway. You get the part, you get fantastic notices, shoot several commercials, decide to move to a huge loft in Soho, and propose to Joanna. You are asked to repeat your part in the film version, and Mr. Mamet tells you there will always be a part for you in all his plays. You see, your future for your character is exactly the same future as you, the actor, desire.

Six Degrees of Separation by John Guare

The actors are Maura and Gil. The characters are OUISA and PAUL. They are on the phone, but we see both actors. PAUL has called her. He had burst into her and her husband's Park Avenue apartment one night recently complaining that he had been stabbed and claiming that he knew OUISA's children from college. He also said he was Sidney Poitier's son. He pleaded for their assistance, which he received, and he proceeded to charm them completely. However, later that night he brought a male lover to the apartment and was caught in the act of lovemaking. They were horrified and threw him and the other young man out. They then discovered that he was not Sidney Poitier's son and did not know their children. He lied to them just to get into a luxury apartment. OUISA is now feeling sorry for him and tells her husband that PAUL just wanted to be "them." She feels that he did more for them in a few hours than their children ever did. PAUL now wants to come back. He wants to be part of her life. He tells her he loves her. She tells him to go to the police, turn himself in, serve his time of a few months, and then she will help him. She knows he's in big trouble, and she is fighting for his trust and for him to remain in her life. I instruct Maura to begin the creative visualization.

OUISA

Ouisa: Paul does as I told him to do. He turns himself in, I appeal on his behalf to the judge, and he gets a suspended sentence. I promise to take him under my wing. We develop a strong and trusting relationship. As a very rich person, I had never been close to someone on such a low economic level, socially. And never with a black man except for the help. I know already how fertile his imagination is, and I now discover how poetic and romantic he is. I gravitate more to him and withdraw from my husband until I realize that I am in love with Paul even though he is young enough to be my son and is black. I find that he is teaching me more about humanity and the meaning of life than I could ever teach him. I make a major move in my life by leaving my husband for Paul. I am fully happy for the first time in my entire life. For the first time I am doing something important.

Ginger: Excellent! I see that you are happy in your new life, but what do you mean you are doing something important?

Ouisa: Well, I am being honest for the first time. I am doing what I want to do, not what I'm supposed to do. I'm seeing the world in a different light. I'm learning about people out there beyond that closed circle of rich and spoiled friends that I was involved with.

Ginger: Fine. Now I am asking you, Maura, can you relate to any of this?

Maura: I certainly can. This is very exciting to me. I

don't come from Ouisa's kind of money or background, but I can understand how such a change in
her life could be so enlightening and rewarding.

Ginger: Maura, tell me what you want your future to
be. Use what excites and turns you on but talk to me
as Ouisa.

Ouisa: Paul and I travel to the great cities around the
world, and we keep a journal of our experiences. We
each see the world in our own eyes and share our
responses and feelings with each other and write all
this in our journal, which we eventually turn into a
giant volume of a book, and we get it published and
it is a best-seller. We write more books on race rela-
tions and being an interracial couple and how we
are accepted in different parts of the world. Our
books become best-sellers.

Ginger: Does this excite you, Maura?

Maura: Yes. I am a writer so I can relate to what
Ouisa is saying.

Ginger: Very good. Continue.

Ouisa: We stay lovers forever, and I am even able to
conceive and have a baby with Paul. I am thrilled to
be having a child at this time in my life. Everything
is perfect in my life.

Ginger: This is what you are fighting for while you
are on the phone with Paul begging him to turn
himself in.

Let's summarize the future. Paul turns himself in,
and you appeal on his behalf to the judge, who gives
him a suspended sentence. You take him under your
wing and develop a loving relationship. You discover his great sense of humanity and romance. For
the first time in your life you feel you are being
honest with your life. You and Paul travel around
the world and keep a journal that eventually turns
into a giant book that is published. You and he write
more books and they all become best-sellers. You
have a child with him and stay lovers forever. *This* is
what you are fighting for.

PAUL

PAUL has been hustling white people all his life. OUISA is the first person he's hustled whom he feels something for. He's finally been caught, and he is in deep trouble. He is fighting for OUISA's love and help. He desperately needs her to be in his life.

Paul: Ouisa decides that I don't have to turn myself in. My crime was against her and her family, and she does not press charges. She meets with me and we talk all night until the sun comes up. I tell her again that I love her. She tells me that she is going to leave her husband. He goes. I move in. Imagine me living on Park Avenue. But don't look at me that way. I really do love this woman. I can't help it if she is filthy rich. I'd love her if she had no money. I probably wouldn't have met her if she wasn't loaded, though. Anyway, I give up hustling and stay put with Ouisa, living the good life.

Ginger: Gil, do you like travel?

Gil: Sure. I haven't done any international travel.

Ginger: If you did, where would you like to visit?

Gil: France, England, Italy, Greece, Russia.

Ginger: Paul, Ouisa and you take an extended trip to Europe. You visit France, England, Italy, Greece, and Russia. Gil, you're an actor. Paul, you've been doing a bang-up job as an actor hustling people practically all your life. How would you like to actually *be* an actor?

Paul: I guess you're right. I have been acting all along. I bet I'd make a terrific actor. Sure. I'd love to.

Ginger: Paul, Ouisa encourages you to take some classes. Tell me what happens.

Paul: I study with a couple of teachers and start to audition. I get cast in a new Bill Cosby TV show in a running part.

Ginger: I assume, Gil, that you would love to be a

regular on a new Cosby show. Paul, now I am asking you this. How is your relationship with Ouisa?

Paul: It's incredible. I never knew I could be so happy and content with one woman. And she seems to want me to have everything. Yeah, we get along fine. Life is good.

Ginger: This is what you are fighting for during that phone conversation with her where she wants you to turn yourself in to the police and you are frantic and frightened.

Let's summarize the future. Ouisa decides that you don't have to turn yourself in. She does not press charges. She meets with you and you talk throughout the night and you tell her how much you love her. Her husband moves out of their Park Avenue apartment, and you move in. You give up hustling and enjoy life with Ouisa. You both take a trip to Europe and visit France, England, Italy, Greece, and Russia. When you return, Ouisa encourages you to study acting. Before long you get a running part in a new Cosby show. You are happier than you've ever been, and you are content to love and be loved by one woman. Life is good for you. *This* is what you are fighting for.

Born Yesterday by Garson Kanin

The actors are Sarah and Joel. The characters are BILLIE and PAUL. BILLIE lives with Harry, a crass, unscrupulous businessman who manipulates her and lets her know how stupid she is. She actually is not stupid at all. She is educationally and culturally deprived. She meets PAUL at a party given by Harry and is so impressed by his mind that Harry hires him to tutor her in the fine arts. He instructs her in art, literature, and history. They meet a couple of times a week. They are very attracted to each other, and she throws out signals to him, but he is not returning them. He would love for her to realize that Harry is a person devoid of humanity and is to be feared.

BILLIE insists that Harry has been good to her and has given her a home and "two mink coats," so how bad could he be? PAUL is trying to teach her about evil and goodness and that she "paid" for those two mink coats; she didn't get them for nothing.

BILLIE

Ginger: So, Billie, you've had a rough life and then Harry came along and gave you a sense of security, a home, and luxury. But he sure made you feel stupid about everything. Paul has been very helpful in the sessions, and now you really have strong feelings toward him, but he seems not to have them for you. In fact, he is the first man who has not come on to you, and it really worries you. See your future as you wish it to be. What do you want to happen immediately after this confrontation with Paul? Don't tell me what you wish could happen; tell me what does happen.

Billie: Paul tells me that he can't hold it in any longer. He loves me and wants me to leave Harry.

Ginger: And then what?

Billie: I am thrilled and I tell him I love him too and we kiss, but I am afraid of what Harry would do to the two of us if I left him for Paul.

Ginger: This is creative visualization. Only positive things happen.

Billie: Okay. I pack my things and have a talk with Harry and he is upset, but he wishes me well.

Ginger: Where do you go?

Billie: Paul takes me to his place.

Ginger: Tell me about his place. Sarah, I am asking you to describe an apartment that would greatly appeal to you. A man's apartment. The man you love.

Sarah: Well, it would be a penthouse with a terrace

overlooking the park. It would be furnished in ultra-modern furniture, and the walls would be covered with fine paintings.

Ginger: This is Paul's apartment. Describe your first evening there, Billie. Sarah, please make choices that are pleasing and exciting to you.

Billie: He opens a bottle of wine, and we sit on the terrace and talk and enjoy the wine and the view. We plan our future. We will live together and get married within a short amount of time. I can continue my studies if I want to by taking classes in whatever area I am interested in.

Ginger: Sarah, I know your passion is acting, but do you have any other skills or interests?

Sarah: Sure. I happen to be a fine pianist. I've been studying since I was nine years old. Well, I don't really study anymore, but I try to practice a few times a week. My mom wanted me to be a concert pianist, but I guess I rebelled and turned to acting. I still love the piano very much.

Ginger: You tell Paul how you always had a good ear for playing, and in fact, Harry even let you take some piano lessons. Now you feel that you would love to get very involved with piano lessons. Paul is delighted and says he will put you in touch with the best piano teacher in the city. Of course, Paul happens to have a baby grand in his living room. Tell me about the rest of the evening.

Billie: We make love for the first time and it is wonderful. With Harry it was always a chore.

Ginger: Sarah, what else can you choose for Billie that would be very meaningful to you?

Sarah: Actually, just living with the man I love in a beautiful apartment with that terrace, studying piano and taking acting classes is just about all I could want at this time. It all appeals to me so much.

Ginger: Billie, this is what you are fighting for today as you and Paul discuss the problems in your life and in the world.

Let's summarize the future. You and Paul finally

confess your love for each other. He asks you to leave Harry and move in with him. You pack, tell Harry, and he wishes you well. Paul's apartment is a penthouse with a terrace furnished in your favorite ultramodern furniture and the walls are covered with fine art. You and he sit on his terrace drinking wine, enjoying the view, and talking of your future together, which includes marriage. You resume your piano studies with his encouragement and your acting classes. You and he live in heavenly bliss. *This* is what you are fighting for.

PAUL

Ginger: Paul, what happens after this confrontation with Billie?

Paul: I have been hesitant about coming on to her because of Harry, but she continues to flirt and be so sexy that I finally kiss her and tell her how I really feel about her and she tells me that she has loved me right from the first time we met. We make plans for her to leave Harry, and I bring her to my place and ask her to stay with me. She does, and for the first time I feel committed to a person.

Ginger: Joel, I'm talking to you. Are you interested in marriage at this time of your life?

Joel: Not really. I've already gone through a marriage, and it wasn't the best time in my life. I'm a little gun shy right now, and marriage is about the last thing I'm interested in. However, I could see myself living with someone.

Ginger: You and Billie live together and put off any talk of marriage. Neither of you is interested in that now. Paul, what kind of work do you do?

Paul: I'm a writer.

Ginger: Joel, can you relate to being a writer?

Joel: Yes, I can. I have written a couple of plays that I
           hope to get produced or I'll produce them myself.
           And I write my monologues. I hope to make it as an
           actor and/or a playwright.

Ginger: Very good. I wish you well. Paul, what kind
           of writing do you do?

Paul: I'm a playwright.

Ginger: A produced playwright?

Paul: Yes. I've written two plays and both have been
           produced off-Broadway. I'm writing my third play.

Ginger: How were the notices?

Paul: Very favorable. In fact, the second one may be
           done as a movie for Jack Nicholson.

Ginger: Joel, I can see that you are very enthusiastic
           about this. What about Billie? Tell me about her
           skills or interests.

Paul: For a while, she sort of settles in and takes care
           of me and the apartment. It's a pleasure not to have
           to do my own laundry and all the household chores,
           which I really detest doing.

Ginger: Joel, is this the way you feel or did you just
           give this to your character?

Joel: This is me! I wish I could have a live-in servant.

Ginger: Well, you've got one, Paul. Only this one is
           beautiful and you and she are in love. How does she
           feel about your writing?

Paul: She read my plays including the one I'm writ-
           ing now, and I'll be damned if she didn't give me
           some very intelligent feedback and ideas to rework
           some of the scenes and improve what I've done!

Ginger: Paul, would you say that life is wonderful
           right now?

Paul: Absolutely. This is perfect. I'm very happy.

Ginger: This is what you are fighting for during your
           confrontation with Billie about the difference be-
           tween evil and good.
              Let's summarize the future. You are a playwright
           and you meet Billie at a party given by her live-in
           boyfriend, who is a crass businessman. You are in-
           stantly attracted to her and Harry asks you to tutor

her in the arts and literature, which you do. You and she get together a couple of times a week for the sessions, and you fall in love with her. She flirts with you, but you hold back because you are fearful of Harry. But you finally confess your love to her, and she admits that she loves you also. She leaves Harry, who does not give either of you a hard time, and she moves in with you. She takes care of you and the apartment and all the chores, and she gives you terrific feedback on the play you are currently writing. She is able to help you in every area of your life. You are very happy. *This* is what you are fighting for.

Everything in the Garden from the play by Giles Cooper, adapted by Edward Albee

The actors are Hope, who is auditioning for JENNY, and Brenda, who is auditioning for MRS. TOOTHE. JENNY is married to Richard and they can barely make ends meet. JENNY desperately tries to keep up with the neighbors. Appearing one day at JENNY's home is MRS. TOOTHE, a stunning Englishwoman who makes JENNY an offer, in a most subtle way, to work for her as a prostitute during the afternoons and earn much money. JENNY is shocked and demands that MRS. TOOTHE leave, but she gives her card to JENNY before she goes. Hope made strong and interesting choices. She is outraged and offended by MRS. TOOTHE's proposition, but she is also excited and flattered. Her love life and romance with her husband leave much to be desired. She has fantasies about having a lover, and she is attracted to the idea of making money. However, she is still mortified by MRS. TOOTHE's audacity. She is fighting for MRS. TOOTHE to care about her and respect her. She must protect JENNY.

JENNY

Jenny: Mrs. Toothe leaves and I calm myself and be-
          gin to think seriously about her offer. Now, I have to
          tell you that as Hope, I have a problem here. How
          can I visualize becoming a whore when the thought
          of doing something like that offends me?

Ginger: In that case, you can't. Forget about making
          such choices. What is it that you want to happen
          next?

Jenny: Mrs. Toothe contacts me again and says that
          she would like to train me to manage the business
          because she has to return to England to take care of
          business matters there. Now, this I can handle. So I
          accept and begin working for her, and I find this
          line of work to be very interesting because all of the
          men who are clients are the leading politicians and
          businessmen in the community and all of the prosti-
          tutes are so-called respectable housewives like I am!
          I earn a lot of money and things improve in my
          marriage and I am able to buy more clothing and
          furniture for the house.

Ginger: Hope, are you able to relate to this at all?

Hope: Sure. This would be a terrific survival job for
          me. I would love to do this kind of work over wait-
          ing tables—that's what I do to pay the rent. I just
          can't relate to being a whore, but I think I could
          handle making appointments for the clients and the
          women and feel okay about that.

Ginger: Good. Now you say you are able to buy
          things now for yourself and for your house that you
          were not able to before. Hope, what do you wish
          you could own that you cannot afford to buy?

Hope: A white iron antique bed, very ornate and old.
          They're over a thousand dollars so it's out of the
          question, but when I have money that's the first
          thing I am going to get for myself.

Ginger: Jenny, the first thing you buy with the money

you are earning is an ornate and old white iron antique bed. Hope, what else do you passionately want?

Hope: My parents' thirty-fifth wedding anniversary is coming up and they've never been to Europe. I wish I could afford to send them to Germany, where they still have relatives, and then France and Italy.

Ginger: Jenny, you earn enough money to send your parents to Europe for their wedding anniversary. Hope, do these things really mean a lot to you? Concentrate on having that bed and seeing the look on your parents' faces when you hand the tickets to them. Do these images excite you, Hope?

Hope: They do. Yes, very much.

Ginger: This is what you are fighting for on the day Mrs. Toothe comes to your house with the intention of having you work for her as a prostitute.

Let's summarize the future. Mrs. Toothe leaves and you begin to think seriously about her offer. She contacts you again and decides that she would like to train you to manage the business. You accept and you love the work. You meet the leading politicians and businessmen in the community, and you earn a lot of money. Your marriage improves. You buy a white iron antique bed and you send your parents to Europe for their wedding anniversary. *This* is what you are fighting for.

MRS. TOOTHE

Mrs. Toothe: Jenny calls me back into the house as I am walking to my car. I return and she informs me that she accepts my offer. I am delighted because she will be my most beautiful girl and I can get more money for her services from the clients. She works out very well. All the men adore her. She brings in more revenue than anyone else ever has.

Ginger: Brenda, does this all offend you?

Brenda: I suppose it should, but for some reason I think this is a hoot, and I have no problem with it.

Ginger: Okay. You're making more money than ever before. Brenda, if you had that kind of money, how would you want to put it to use?

Brenda: I would love to have my own acting company and produce plays right here in New York and also tour with them around the country.

Ginger: Mrs. Toothe, you earn enough money through the business to save and invest, which brings more revenue. Jenny takes over running the business so you can go forth and fulfill a lifetime dream. You start an acting company and produce plays. Your productions are very well received. You are successful in your production company. Brenda, would you want to perform in these plays?

Brenda: Yes. Not all the plays. Just when a great part comes up for my age range.

Ginger: Mrs. Toothe, you perform in the plays that have wonderful parts for your age range. Brenda, does the thought and visualization of this kind of life really excite and stimulate you?

Brenda: It sounds like heaven on earth. It's exactly what I dream of.

Ginger: Mrs. Toothe, this is what you are fighting for on that day you visit Jenny to offer her a job.

Let's summarize the future. Jenny accepts your offer. Because of her great beauty she brings in more revenue than anyone else has. You are earning more money now so you make a lifelong dream come true. You start an acting company that is based in New York and you play many parts. You tour around the country. Jenny takes over running your business. *This* is what you are fighting for.

Equus by Peter Shaffer

The actors are John, who is auditioning for DR. DYSART, and Anna, who is auditioning for HESTER. DR. DYSART, a psychiatrist, is talking to HESTER, a court administrator, about himself and his young patient, Alan, who has blinded six horses. The doctor reveals to HESTER that his life and marriage have been barren and devoid of passion. He laments the irony that Alan is called insane and he, the doctor, is called sane. At least, he feels, Alan *did* what he wanted to do! HESTER is alarmed by this statement. He tells her that he hasn't kissed his wife in six years. Now, there is nothing on the audition sides to indicate that the doctor and HESTER love each other, or for that matter, that they have a close relationship; but the actors, John and Anna, each chose to love the other.

HESTER

As soon as HESTER heard the doctor speak of the lack of love in his marriage, she felt encouraged that there might be a chance for her in his life. She also made choices that she was extremely frightened for him and that his radical talk could endanger his professional and personal future. He might be having a breakdown. Anna made intelligent choices and got a callback. I instruct Anna to begin the creative visualization.

Hester: After listening to the doctor share his personal life and his innermost thoughts with me, I speak up with all my courage and declare my love for him and plead with him to allow me into his life so that I can help him. He throws his arms around me and reveals his love for me! He says he has loved me since he first saw me but didn't dare communicate it, but now—what the hell! He says he is going to leave his wife and already he begins to put things into perspective regarding himself and Alan.

Ginger: Good. And then what happens?

Hester: He does leave his wife. He moves in with me. Life is bliss. I have loved him for so long, and we are finally together. He continues to treat Alan, and the boy comes around. He changes drastically and eventually is able to function and get on with his life. Richard (Dr. Dysart's first name) becomes famous because of this case and writes a book that is published and becomes a best-seller. A Hollywood film is made, based on the book, and it wins the Academy Award.

Ginger: And then what?

Anna: I would like to use something that really is very personal from my own life at this time.

Ginger: That's the whole idea. Go on.

Anna: As much as I want to make it as a professional actor working on Broadway and doing films some-day, there is something else I crave. I've been mar-ried twelve years, and for the last five years we have been trying to have a baby, but we haven't been successful. I would like to choose, as Hester, that I become pregnant and we have a child. If I am sup-posed to bring the strongest creative visualization to the preparation, this would be it.

Ginger: By all means use this! I don't believe your choice will be detrimental to your mental situation. After all, it is very positive. You're not dealing with the failure to conceive.

Hester: Richard and I discover we are going to have a baby. We are beyond thrilled. I cannot express how joyous this news is for us.

Ginger: This is what you are fighting for as he is tell-ing you about his barren life and his concerns about his sanity.

Let's summarize the future. You declare your love for him and plead with him to allow you to help him. He confesses that he has loved you since he first met you. He leaves his wife and he begins to put things into perspective regarding himself and Alan. You live together happily. He gets on with his life and cures Alan. He writes a book about the case, which becomes a best-seller. Hollywood buys the book and it becomes an Academy Award–winning movie. You then discover you are pregnant and you both are ecstatic. *This* is what you are fighting for.

DR. DYSART

John also made the choice that it was HESTER that he was in love with and he desperately needed her to help him to survive and change his life. He incorporated the irony and absurdity of his statement about Alan's and his mental state into his performance by simply being aware of how absurd his life is. I instruct John to begin the creative visualization.

Dr. Dysart: I need Hester to save me. I feel like I am drowning.

Ginger: That was before creative visualization. Yes, you certainly do feel this way and she *must* save you. That is what you are fighting for. Now I want you to take it further. Tell me what occurs immediately after this conversation. What do you want to happen? What do you want her to do? To say?

Dr. Dysart: I want her to say that she loves me.

Ginger: You don't have to tell me that you *want* her to say that. She *says* it to you. Now tell me, what does she say to you?

Dr. Dysart: She tells me that she loves me and wants to help me. She tells me how brilliant and wonderful I am and how I am helping Alan. She tells me that I deserve a better life than the one I have with my wife. She tells me how she and I could live an exciting life together. Then I confess that I have always loved her and we kiss. For the first time in my entire life, I feel alive and vital as a man. We talk for hours and hold each other and make plans for our future. I feel validated as a doctor, and I see things more clearly regarding Alan and myself. We have dinner together and when I take her home, we make love with great passion. I feel reborn.

Ginger: What is the next big event in your life?

Dr. Dysart: I break up my marriage, and Hester and I live together in utter bliss. I continue my work with Alan and get him on the road to recovery.

Ginger: John, what are your major interests in life other than acting?

John: I love sailing. Been doing it since I was a kid. My father had a boat, and we were on it every day during the summer. I enjoy painting. It's a hobby that I don't get to do much of these days. In fact, I rarely get to go sailing.

Ginger: If you had the time and could afford it, where would you like to sail?

John: I'd spend the summer sailing the Mediterranean from Italy to France to Spain. Maybe through the Greek islands.

Ginger: Dr. Dysart, you and Hester sail the Mediterranean throughout the entire summer. John, are you now or have you ever been completely in love?

John: I have been. I'm divorced and not romantically involved at this time.

Ginger: Can you draw on an experience and relationship you have had in the past when you were in love?

John: Sure. I can remember.

Ginger: Remember well. I want you to draw on that feeling and bring it to the audition stage because this is what you are fighting for: sailing the Mediterranean with the woman you love.

Let's summarize the future. Hester admits that she loves you. She tells you how brilliant and wonderful you are and how you are helping Alan. She says you deserve a better life and marriage. You confess that you love her. She helps you to see things more clearly. You have dinner together and then make love with great passion. You divorce your wife. You get Alan on the road to recovery. You and Hester sail the Mediterranean throughout the entire summer. You finally are doing what you truly want to do. *This* is what you are fighting for.

On Golden Pond by Ernest Thompson

The actors are Gary, who is auditioning for BILL, and Robert, who is auditioning for NORMAN. BILL is having a serious relationship with NORMAN and Ethel's daughter, Chelsea. They have just arrived at her parents' summer home in the woods at Golden Pond to drop off BILL's son, Billy, by a former marriage. He will stay with Chelsea's parents while she and BILL vacation in Europe. NORMAN is a snappy, testy curmudgeon. Chelsea has forewarned BILL about him and now BILL is attempting to have a discussion with him. He wants permission to sleep in the same bed with Chelsea and soon realizes that NORMAN is up to his old tricks in his answers. Gary made strong choices to get NORMAN to like him and make him feel welcome. Robert's strong choices were to test BILL to see if he was manful and spirited enough for his daughter. I instruct Gary to begin the creative visualization.

BILL

Bill: Our conversation has me in a situation of frustration because had it been anyone other than Chelsea's dad, I would have told him off. Although I must admit, he's got spunk and humor. Well anyway, he begins to laugh, and he tells me he was just putting me on and that I shouldn't feel badly because he really likes me, and he says how Chelsea has told him how much she loves me. So I feel much better. He also says that it's fine with him if Chelsea and I sleep in the same bed in his house. It's important that he really likes me because I had a father from hell. It was really bad, and I would like to get close to Norman.

Ginger: Well, you do. That's what you want, therefore that's what you get in creative visualization. Tell me, Gary, did you have a good relationship with your father or did you really have an abusive father.

Gary: I really did. He drank and was a madman to me and my mom. That's why I made the choice. Why not? That makes me want and need Norman all the more.

Ginger: Excellent! So many of us had difficulties with our parents, but we must draw on those circumstances and events for performance. What happens next?

Bill: Norman and I become great friends. Chelsea and I marry and Norman becomes a positive and influencing force in my life.

Ginger: This is what you are fighting for on the day that you first meet Norman and he gives you a hard time.

Let's summarize the future. After your conversation with Norman, he tells you he was just putting you on and that you shouldn't feel badly. He also says it's fine if you and Chelsea share a bed in his house. You and Norman become close friends. You and Chelsea marry, and Norman remains a positive influence in your life. He becomes your father! *This* is what you are fighting for.

NORMAN

Norman: I like Bill. He stands up to me. Doesn't take my crap. Chelsea was married before to a six-foot-two twelve-year-old! His mind got stuck in that age. It broke my heart when she broke up with him. Oh, I was glad she was rid of him, but she was in a bad way. She seemed to love that misfit. But this one! Bill. He seems to have what it takes. I test him out. He's a man! Also, I never had a son. Always regretted it. Well, I may have one now. As a matter of fact, if I had one, I wouldn't mind if he turned out just like Bill.

Ginger: Good. What happens next?

Norman: I let him sleep in the damn bed with my daughter. We spend a few days with them. He and I go fishing and we talk about everything important in the world. As a matter of fact, I start to feel more mentally alert. Bill gets my thinking going. We play cards and chess and we talk about baseball; and unlike Ethel and Chelsea he's interested in hearing all about the great ones who played in my time. He really gets me going. I feel better than I've felt in years. I give them a wedding. Not too big or grand but nice. Bill talks Chelsea into living near us. I'm very happy about having my children near me. Now I've got everything I want.

Ginger: Robert, how can you relate to this?

Robert: Well, I don't know. I've got two grown sons and a daughter. They're all married and two of them live in the Northeast, so I get to see them often, and one lives in Arizona, so I only see him about once or twice a year. I lost my wife two years ago. I have no interest in having a serious relationship with a woman. My career is what I am interested in more than anything. I'm retired. I have money. I don't have to work to support myself. You tell me. How do I relate to this?

Ginger: Let's not look for anything esoteric. How would you feel if all your children lived far from you instead of just one?

Robert: I wouldn't like that. I'm grateful that two are close enough. Especially because of my grandson. He's named for me, and he's pretty special.

Ginger: So little Robert is very important in your life, and knowing you're close to your children means a lot to you.

Robert: Absolutely!

Ginger: Continue.

Robert: I think I need a little help here. Where do I go from here?

Ginger: All right. Just visualize that all your children live in the Northeast, not just two of them. See yourself with them all on holidays and in between the holidays too. Think of all the things you enjoy doing and do them with your kids and your grandson. Having them see you in a Broadway play or all of you sitting in a movie house watching you on the screen. Of course, Norman is not an actor, but use this to evoke strong and positive feelings for yourself. As Norman you are fighting for closeness and love and friendship from Bill throughout the remainder of your life. And when Bill and Chelsea have a child, he or she will be named for you and will be close to you forever.

Let's summarize the future. You like Bill. He stands up to you. He's a man! You never had a son. If you had had one, it would be just fine with you if he had turned out just like Bill. You go fishing with him and the two of you have stimulating conversations, which gets your thinking going, and you start to feel more mentally alert. You and he play cards and chess, and he's interested in everything you have to say about baseball in the old days. You throw them a wedding. Bill talks Chelsea into living near you. When they have a son, they name him after you. You are surrounded by your loved ones. *This* is what you are fighting for.

The Lisbon Traviata by Terrence McNally

The actors are Scott, auditioning for STEPHEN, and Kerry, auditioning for MIKE. They have been lovers for eight years, but MIKE has started a new relationship and is no longer interested in continuing with STEPHEN, who he feels killed the love because of his coolness and indifference. STEPHEN is begging him not to leave him and MIKE is trying to explain why he must. Both actors fought with every ounce of emotional energy within them. I instruct Scott to begin the creative visualization.

STEPHEN

Stephen: He finally comes around and says he will stay. I promise him I will change if he will help me to. He tells his new friend that he won't be seeing him anymore, and we work things out between us. I realize how much I love him and need him in my life, and I am sort of glad that we went through this crisis because our relationship becomes stronger than ever.

Ginger: Very good. Can you relate to this situation, Scott?

Scott: To tell you the truth, I've got a little problem with it because I am not gay.

Ginger: You don't have to be gay to play gay. Love is love! For the sake of the audition and cold reading, substitute and personalize. Use a woman as you are preparing and making your choices, but once you are performing the scene at the audition, you must play off the writer's script, and this one deals with the love between two men. You say you have a little problem because you are not gay, but you gave a strong and convincing performance at the cold reading, so I don't see where you have a problem. Tell

me, Scott, have you ever been in a situation similar
to the one between these two people? After all, their
problem is not a gay or straight problem. It can exist
in any relationship.

Scott: I've got a great girlfriend. We've been together
about eight months and we get along terrific.

Ginger: I'm glad. What are your plans and goals for
the future of the two of you?

Scott: Well, we just took an apartment together, and
we're not too keen on getting married until at least
one of us makes it. We both want to get to Broadway
and then films. We want the same things.

Ginger: Give this goal to your characters. The playwright has not indicated what Stephen and Mike do
for a living, so you might as well make them actors.
If he had given them a specific profession, you
could still make them actors. Stephen, you and
Mike continue to audition, and one after the other,
you get cast in Broadway shows. You get wonderful
notices, and before long you are auditioning for and
get cast in your first film. Mike follows soon after.
The two of you enjoy a wonderful life of acting in
films and loving each other. This is what you are
fighting for.

Let's summarize the future. Mike finally agrees to
stay. He gives up his new friend, and together you
make your relationship stronger than ever. You are
both actors and good ones. You start getting parts on
Broadway and film. *This* is what you are fighting for.

MIKE

Kerry understood that STEPHEN is the most important
person in his life, not his new lover, and he made intelligent inner life choices. He chose to be lying to STE-
PHEN about caring for the new man. He was actually still
in love with STEPHEN and was trying once and for all to

get him to wake up and change, to be less casual and more involved and active in their relationship, and to really listen, hear, and respond to him, not just take him for granted. He also is tired of being everything to him with very little returned. I instruct Kerry to begin the creative visualization.

Mike: Stephen convinces me to give him another chance. I stay and break off with Paul. I never stopped loving Stephen, but he lived in his damned operas, listening to them more than to me; but now he changes and becomes more accessible, and this is what I wanted all along. Now he is loving to me, and we are very happy together once more.

Ginger: Very good. Kerry, have you ever been hurt in love?

Kerry: More than once.

Ginger: Then you can draw on your own experiences. Just make sure the trauma is resolved. What kind of things do you enjoy doing with a loved one?

Kerry: Are you asking me or the character?

Ginger: You, Kerry.

Kerry: I like to bike through Central Park. I like to try new restaurants. I love to go to the theater and see just about any movie. I love to go away to a warm beach in the winter. I like us to read books side by side by a fireplace. I like to cook Indian food for him.

Ginger: These are the things you are fighting for today as you are telling him that you are leaving him.

Let's summarize the future. Stephen convinces you to give him another chance, and you do because you still love him very much. He changes and becomes more accessible to you. He is very loving. The two of you do all the things you love to do that he never before had enough time for. You bike through Central Park, try new restaurants, go to the theater, and see every movie playing in New York. You spend a couple of weeks in the West Indies in the winter and you sit side by side in front of your fireplace reading and you cook great Indian food. *This* is what you are fighting for.

The Ladies of the Corridor
by Dorothy Parker and Arnaud D'Usseau

Margo is auditioning for the part of LULU and Leslie for the part of CONNIE. LULU is expecting Paul for dinner, but once again he is late. While she waits CONNIE shows up with exciting news about her business trip to Europe. LULU is devastated by Paul's indifference to her and confesses to her friend how desperate she is to have this younger man love her and marry her. CONNIE proposes that LULU accompany her to Europe, but LULU declines. CONNIE is very concerned about her good friend.

LULU

Lulu: Connie convinces me to go to Europe with her. As much as I hate leaving Paul, I go. After all, he has been so distant to me anyway. So we go off and we have a really great time.

Ginger: Margo, tell me the cities in Europe you would most love to visit.

Margo: Paris, Rome, Venice, Florence, London, Copenhagen, Amsterdam, Vienna.

Ginger: Lulu, you visit Paris, Rome, Venice, Florence, London, Copenhagen, Amsterdam, Vienna. Tell me more.

Lulu: I meet men wherever we go, and I have a couple of flings. It's wonderful to be free and not so dependent on one man for his attention and his love. The men I meet in Europe all treat me wonderfully. And when we get to London, guess what? I meet someone very special who I really fall in love with and he with me. Now I find out for the first time in my life what love and a relationship is supposed to be. He asks me to marry him, and I accept. And this all came about because of Connie. Without her I would have languished back home. We get married and Connie is my maid of honor. I am happy for the first time in my life with a wonderful man who appreciates me and loves me. Connie gets to take a lot of business trips to London, so we get to see each other several times a year. And I travel back to the States also a couple of times a year. Life is great.

Ginger: This is what you are fighting for from Connie on this evening when she shows up instead of Paul.

Let's summarize the future. Connie convinces you to go to Europe with her and forget about Paul. You have a great time there. You visit Paris, Rome, Venice, Florence, London, Copenhagen, Amsterdam, and Vienna. You meet lots of men along the way and have a few flings. In London you meet the love of your life. You and he marry, and you live in London with him. Connie gets to visit you a few times a year, and you travel to the States a couple of times a year. *This* is what you are fighting for.

CONNIE

Connie: I don't want to go to Europe without Lulu. She is in a very bad way, and I won't be able to concentrate and enjoy my trip knowing that I would be leaving her in her current state. So I simply tell her I will not go without her. Of course, Paul doesn't show up at all, so I just stay over for the night and we do a lot of talking and, by early morning, she agrees to come with me. I love her very much, and what she doesn't realize is that I love her romantically. I've never told her and I've never done anything, but it's true. So I'm ecstatic that we'll be traveling together for a few months. I'll have plenty of time for her after my meetings with clients.

Ginger: Don't say, "I'll." Say "I." Take me along on your visualization. Go from one event to another.

Connie: We do have a marvelous time. I show her how life can be wonderful without a man. I take her to beautiful places. Romantic places. We stay in the finest hotels and eat in the best and most beautiful restaurants. I court her like a man would do, but I don't come on to her. Until late in the trip, it appears as if she might be receptive, and I say something to her. Although she is surprised, she is not repulsed or angry. Eventually, we do become lovers, and finally this woman who I have known for almost all of my adult life as a true and kind friend is now my lover. I am overjoyed.

Leslie: And yes, Ginger, I am gay so I can relate well to this. That's why I made these choices.

Ginger: This is what you are fighting for as she cries to you over Paul not loving her.

Let's summarize the future. You don't want to go to Europe and leave Lulu. She needs you, and you would not only miss her but worry about her also. She agrees to accompany you by early morning. She does not know that you are in love with her. In Europe you take her to the finest places, and you both have a wonderful time. Late in the trip, you suddenly get the feeling that she might just be receptive to you, so you say something to her about being gay and she is cool about it. Eventually you become lovers and both of you are very happy. *This* is what you are fighting for.

Agnes of God by **John Pielmeier**

Peggy is auditioning for the part of AGNES, a young nun, and Alice is auditioning for the DOCTOR. The DOCTOR is attempting to get AGNES to face her traumatic childhood and remember the events that recently led to the murder of a newborn infant found in the wastepaper basket in AGNES's room in the convent after being delivered by her.

AGNES

Agnes: The doctor tells me that everything is going to be all right and not to worry or be sad. She asks me if I would like to visit her in her apartment, and I say I would. She gets permission from Mother Superior, and we go to her place. It is very pretty and bright. She tells me all about herself and what her childhood was like and doesn't probe any more into my past. We actually have a good time together and even laugh together. I love her very much. She is like a mother to me, at least like I know how a mother is supposed to be. She asks me if I would like to spend more time at her place with her and I say yes, so once again she gets the permission and I move in. She takes me places and buys me things, and she cares about me. But I am a nun, and eventually I want to get back to the convent to continue doing the work of God. Somehow she makes everything all right and I feel safe and at peace, and I am able to return to the convent. She visits me often and tells me that I am the daughter she never had. I am very grateful to her for helping me, and I live my life doing the work I want to do. For the first time, I am happy. All due to the doctor.

Ginger: Peggy, how can you relate to this?

Peggy: I can't.

Ginger: I didn't think so. There are very few actors who aspire to becoming a nun. I want you to personalize this so that for the creative visualization, you are enthusiastic about your future—as *Peggy*. Remember, if there is a problem, there is a solution. Let's find it. I can't see Agnes wishing to enter the theater world any more than you wish to become a nun and relinquish the outside world. So it is my opinion that when you move into the doctor's place, you decide eventually that you no longer wish to be a nun. Tell me what your strongest interests are aside from acting.

Peggy: Writing music, playing my guitar, getting my songs published, singing them in clubs, on video, on TV, being with my cats and filling my apartment with more, eventually having a large house in the country and taking in every stray cat I can find.

Ginger: All right. That is plenty to work with. Agnes, you live with the doctor, she becomes the mother you wish you had, you make a decision to leave the convent, and you discover with the doctor's guitar that you have musical talent. She teaches you to play. Before long, you are hearing melodies in your head that you play. You put words to the music. This gives you immeasurable pleasure, and one day you audition for a local club. They love you and your music and you begin to play there. Eventually a record producer comes in, and he also loves your music and you start to record. Your songs get a lot of air time, and you earn a healthy amount of money. You do videos, you sing on TV, you score films, and you earn enough to buy a large house in the country and take in and care for stray cats. Does this excite you, Peggy?

Peggy: Yes. It sounds great.

Ginger: Then this is what you are fighting for as the doctor talks to you and probes for information about your unhappy childhood.

Let's summarize the future. The doctor convinces

you that everything will be all right. She gets permission from Mother Superior for you to visit her. You and she have a wonderful time. She is like the mother you wish you could have had. You make a decision to leave the convent, and you move in with the doctor. You begin playing her guitar and realize that you have musical talent and love playing. She teaches you to play, and you begin to write songs. One day you audition for a local club, and they love you and your music and you play there. A record producer comes in, hears you, and signs you to do a record. You begin to earn money from your record. You do videos, sing on television, and score films. You buy a large house in the country and take in and care for stray cats. *This* is what you are fighting for.

DOCTOR

Doctor: I am able to break through to her and she reveals the horrors of her childhood and admits that her mother was a monster. This is a great release for her. As for the investigation into the death of the infant, there are no charges made against her. I am thrilled that the horror is now over, but now I want to treat her to make sure that she is free to make adult and healthy choices for herself in her life. I counsel her in therapy for several months and learn to love her very much.

Ginger: How does this affect your life, Doctor?

Doctor: Well, I never married and have no children. Agnes makes me feel like a mother. I want to mother her all the time. I like the feeling.

Ginger: What about your career? How does this all influence your future work?

Doctor: Word gets around how well I handled this case. I am asked to write a book and am offered a large amount of money to do it. But I consult with Agnes about how she would feel about such a book. We discuss it and she decides that such a book might be very important for others who went through what she went through as a child, and as for what occurred at the convent, she felt she could handle it. Her name would not be used. So I write it and it becomes a best-seller.

Ginger: Tell me, Doctor, does Hollywood by any chance buy the book to make into a major film?

Doctor: I suppose so.

Ginger: What do you mean, "I suppose so?" Of course it does! You are a very attractive woman and you have wonderful communication skills. Who do they want to play the doctor?

Doctor: Me?

Ginger: Yes. You. Isn't that terrific? Now tell me more about Agnes. Does she stay at the convent?

Doctor: That is her wish. I am very happy for her. I visit her often and they allow her to visit me. I truly feel I have a daughter.

Ginger: Alice, how do you relate to all this?

Alice: I don't have a daughter. I have two sons, but I always wished I could have a girl. I am Catholic, so I can appreciate the convent and her wish to be a nun, although it's not what I would want to do. But as a girl I went through the experience of dreaming of becoming a nun one day. That was gone as soon as I noticed boys. I am not a doctor, but I am always counseling everyone in the family. I don't write, but I read a lot and I envy anyone who has the discipline to write books and get them published. I relate to earning a large sum of money. Not that I have, but I aspire to it. And, of course, starring in a major film is what I would kill for.

Ginger: This is what you are fighting for as you are questioning Agnes.

Let's summarize the future. You break through to her and she reveals the horrors of her childhood to you. No charges are made against her. You are her therapist for several months, and you learn to love her very much. You love the feeling of mothering her. You are asked to write a book about the case. After consulting with Agnes, she encourages you to write it, which you do, and it becomes a best-seller. It is made into a major film and you play the doctor. Agnes happily returns to the convent, and you and she are still able to see each other quite frequently. You have fame, money, and the daughter you never had. *This* is what you are fighting for.

At this time I want you to practice creative visualization by turning to Chapter 1, reading the dialogue of Nora or Helmer in *A Doll's House,* and then preparing for the cold reading and for your callback. Make your choices from *your* head, *your* world, and *your* sensibilities. You are familiar with the choices made in this book, and perhaps you are familiar with the entire play. Now it is time to create your choices. You certainly are free to choose another play if you wish. This kind of work requires no partner. You may quite successfully practice preparation for the initial audition and for the callback on your own. After you have made your choices, get a friend or family member to be your reader.

You are on your own each and every time you audition.

ABOUT THE AUTHOR

GINGER HOWARD FRIEDMAN is the author of the highly-acclaimed *The Perfect Monologue*. She has been a Broadway, off-Broadway, television and film casting director for several years. She has directed on cable television and in regional theatre and is a produced playwright and an actress. She has been teaching her popular "How to Audition/ Rehearse" classes in New York and Los Angeles since 1976. Ginger travels throughout the U.S. and Canada presenting her workshops for college theatre departments. Her videotapes on auditioning are used in universities throughout the country.

Ginger is the founder of the Actors' Audition Institute. She is currently based in Toronto, teaching at her school and at several actors' talent agencies. She also teaches presentation and communication skills to politicians, lawyers and businesspeople.

Ginger is a strong defender of animal rights.